in over our heads

# { in over our heads }

## meditations on grace

by William R. White

Augsburg Fortress
MINNEAPOLIS

IN OVER OUR HEADS
Meditations on Grace

Large-quantity purchases or custom editions of this book are available at a discount from the publisher. For more information contact the sales department at Augsburg Fortress, 1-800-328-4648 or write to: Sales Director, Augsburg Fortress, Box 1209, Minneapolis, MN 55440-1209.

*Library of Congress Cataloging-in-Publication Data*
White, William R. (William Robert), 1939-
  In over our heads : meditations on grace / by William R. White.
     p. cm.
  Includes bibliographical references.
  ISBN-13: 978-0-8066-9059-9 (pbk. : alk. paper)
  1. Christian life—Meditations. I. Title.
  BV4501.3.W4675 2007
  242—dc22      2007002001

Cover design by Kevin Van Der Leek
Cover photo © Ralph A. Clevenger/CORBIS. Used by permission.
Book design by Michelle L. N. Cook

Manufactured in the U.S.A.

11    10    09    08    07        1    2    3    4    5    6    7    8    9    10

# { contents }

*And so here I am, preaching and writing*
*about things that are way over my head,*
*the inexhaustible riches and generosity of Christ.*
—*Ephesians 3:9,* The Message

# { introduction }

One day early in my first year as a pastor, a young woman called to make an appointment. She told me that she was visiting her parents and wanted to talk. When she arrived she immediately began to tell an amazing story. About three years earlier she and her sister were married in a double wedding. The night before the ceremony, their hair in curlers, lying on their childhood bed, the two sisters made a confession. One said, "Some time ago I realized this marriage will never work. The only reason I haven't cancelled is I haven't wanted to disappoint you."

Her sister let out a shriek and said, "Me too!"

A year after the double wedding there was a double divorce.

Some time later my visitor gave birth to a child fathered by a second man whom she neither married nor lived with. Later she moved in with a third male who was separated from his wife. There was more, but by now you have the general pattern. Her story took nearly forty minutes to tell.

As she spoke I sat in silence trying my best not to look astonished, which I was. When she stopped talking I couldn't think of a single thing to say. Though I silently prayed, "God, help me," not a word came out of my mouth. I was twenty-five years old and clearly in over my head.

Finally, she broke the silence by saying, "Thank you so much pastor. You have no idea how much this has helped me." She walked toward the door, put her hand on the knob and said, "I didn't miss your gentle reminder that I need to practice my faith. I'll be at worship this weekend."

As soon as her car left the driveway I ran up the steps from my basement parsonage office to my wife, and said, "What just happened?" After a long conversation we both agreed I had experienced a grace moment.

As I look back I realize that my forty-two years as a pastor are filled with grace moments, experiences when I have been rescued from my lack of skill, intelligence, and insight by a loving and merciful God. I have received far more than I have given. There is no doubt that I have been a recipient of people's forgiveness more than I have been a bearer of it.

These lines from the hymn "Amazing Grace" may well summarize my ministry:

*Through many dangers, toils, and snares I have already come;*
*'Tis grace has brought me safe thus far, and grace will lead me*
*home.*

I am thankful for my life as a pastor. Not only do I enjoy preaching, teaching, and counseling, I get a thrill out of tackling new pieces of ministry that are challenging. Three experiences stand out:

• working to integrate two Bible camps by hiring six black counselors and recruiting one hundred fifty black campers during my third year as director.

• leaving a congregation where I was the only pastor for a church where I was called to supervise a staff of thirty-four, including five other pastors.

• helping to convince a congregation I served that the best way to celebrate our Norwegian past was to again become a bilingual congregation, using Spanish as our second language for worship.

In each case I was in over my head. In each case I learned, "'Tis grace has brought me safe thus far, and grace will lead me home." Since I live by and rely on grace, it is not surprising that it has became the dominant theme for my preaching and teaching.

During my time as a pastor I have served in both rural and urban churches. In two congregations most of the people earned their living by farming. Only a handful had attended college. Two other congregations have been in university towns, where many of the members of the church earned the title, "Dr."

I have discovered that farmers and university professors, small town folk and big town folk, have far more in common than most people assume. They all face challenges in their marriages, problems raising their children, and difficulties relating to their parents and siblings. They all have friends that die too soon, acquaintances that drink too much, and children who face an uncertain future. Nearly everyone has failed to become what they once dreamed they would be. Each is in need of God's love and forgiveness. Each finds grace amazing and wonderful.

All of the chapters in this book have had a previous life. Some were birthed as sermons, others as Bible lessons, and still others as newsletter articles. With a little help from my friends they have been reshaped to fit this book.

Many of my ideas are result from conversations with my colleagues—Katie Baardseth, Duane Hanson, Gary Lewis, Jacqui Shanda, Pedro Suarez, John Swanson, and my office partner Marian Osterberg. Suzzane Alexander was kind enough to read the manuscript and make suggestions. I am grateful to all of them.

My greatest debt belongs to my best friend and life companion, Sally. Through many dangers, toils, and snares we have already come . . . together. She understands grace as well as anyone and lives it each day.

—Bill White

# part one

forgiveness

# { as we forgive }

*And forgive us our debts,*
*as we also have forgiven our debtors.*
*For if you forgive others their trespasses, your heavenly Father will*
*also forgive you; but if you do not forgive others, neither will your*
*Father forgive your trespasses.*
        —*Matthew 6:12, 14-15*

One chilly evening eighty-eight-year-old Heddie Braun, who stands 5'2" and weighs eighty pounds soaking wet and swinging both arms, was kidnapped from her single-story home in Little Prairie, near Whitewater, Wisconsin, where she lived with her blind husband, Eddie. Eddie, who was asleep when the kidnapper broke in, didn't miss her until the next morning. The adventure began when the kidnapper cut the wires to the house. Heddie had no idea how the lights went off and decided that if she couldn't see she might as well go to bed. She went into the bedroom and put on her slippers and a nightgown. Suddenly the kidnapper entered through the back door, picked her up, and carried her to the trunk of his '92 Cadillac. He drove her to his home, put chains on her legs, and laid her in a tiny trailer behind his house. He lit a kerosene heater to provide some relief from the frigid February weather and left a few blankets. In the next few days he came by infrequently to bring a hamburger and some orange juice.

The morning after her capture the kidnapper gave Heddie a disposable cell phone and ordered her to speak to her grandson at the family construction company. The newspaper article said such a phone is almost impossible to trace. Heddie, who is nearly deaf, didn't understand the kidnapper's instructions, and the grandson who received the call didn't know at the time his grandmother was missing. The phone call was a total failure.

When at last Heddie was missed, her relatives thought she had left the house to visit friends. Later, evidence of a break-in was discovered and the police began to suspect something dreadful had happened.

Two days after she was kidnapped, a ransom note appeared demanding $3 million in cash from her family. The FBI was called in and the sheriff's department went on full alert.

Meanwhile, things were getting worse for Heddie. She was chilled to the bone, she didn't have her heart medicine, and in the darkness of the tiny trailer she lost track of time. Her slippers fell off her feet and ice encrusted on the chains around her ankles. Though she knew she couldn't last much longer, she didn't feel bitter or frightened. The newspaper reports that she only felt grateful–grateful her abductor hadn't beaten or raped her.

Eddie calls Heddie, who lived the first four years of her life in Norway, "My Tough Norwegian." Her toughness certainly helped in her survival.

Though she was confused about the time, she was not confused about who she was and who she belonged to. She had been to church the previous Sunday. She was at peace with her family and her Lord. If necessary, she was ready to die.

By now the police and the FBI began looking at numbers from the phone company's disposable phones. Slowly, they sorted through thousands of numbers and suddenly identified a suspect. It was a man who had worked for Heddie's family. Fortunately, the suspect was a friend of one of the policemen. They knew he'd had a previous scrape with the law. The police set up surveillance and finally at 11:45 A.M. on the fourth day, as he drove along Interstate 43, thirty unmarked police cars stopped the kidnapper's vehicle and confronted him. He confessed and told them where to find Heddie. The kidnapper said to a police-man, "I was desperate." He had put the scheme together after losing his $32-an-hour job.

When they found her, someone said, "You're safe now."

She whispered, "What took you so long?"

At first it appeared that the frostbite was so severe that she would lose her left foot, but she was tough and the foot was saved. When asked how she stayed strong she replied, "I'm Norwegian."

What happened next is the point of this story. Heddie told everyone, "I forgive him." Then to her daughter, "You have to, too."

The author of a four-part article distributed by the Associ-ated Press, Helen O'Neill, said: "But forgiveness was hard as the family listened in court to the rambling apology of a man they once considered a friend."

The truth is forgiveness is always hard. It's not easy to give up your right to get even. It isn't easy to give up revenge, and it is especially difficult to give up hatred for a person who mistreats your eighty-eight-year-old grandmother.

Heddie said the whole time she was in the trailer she tried to remember that the kidnaper was a person just like her. Heddie had been to church enough to know we are commanded by our Lord to forgive. Forgiveness is a choice, but if you are a serious disciple of Jesus it is the only good choice.

In 1981, Pope John Paul II was struck with three bullets while being driven in a convertible through St. Peter's Square in Rome where twenty-thousand people had gathered to see him. He was rushed to the hospital where he barely survived a six-hour operation.

The would-be assassin, twenty-three year old Turkish terror-ist Mehmet Ali Agca, was apprehended on the spot and placed in prison. In his pockets they found several notes in Turkish. One of them read, "I am killing the Pope as a protest against the imperialism of the Soviet Union and the United States."

Shortly after he got out of the hospital the Pope visited his would-be assassin in his prison cell and told him he forgave him. Later, he met with the man's mother and told her he would support her efforts to move her son to Turkey. A few days later he explained to some children that Christ instructed him to forgive even his enemies. He asked others to pray, "for the brother who shot me, the brother I have sincerely forgiven." Like many commands of Jesus, forgiveness is hard, but vital.

The disciples of Jesus came to him and asked him: "Teach us to pray." Most rabbis who had a following in the first century taught their disciples a prayer that summarized their teaching. The request of the disciples was not just a request to know how to pray, but what to pray. It was a request to understand the teaching of Jesus. The Lord's Prayer gave them what they asked for.

Jews during the time of Jesus often began their prayers by saying, "O Great God, king of the Universe." However, Jesus said, "When you pray, say, Our Father in Heaven." Simple and to the point. The notion of God as father was so much a part of the understanding and practice of Jesus that a German theologian has said, "If you pray using any other name for God than Father you are praying to a different God than the one Jesus prayed to."

Often, Jesus used the word Abba, which we translate as father. Abba sounds similar to a word children use to speak to their father—daddy, or dada. Martin Luther explained, "Here God encourages us to believe that he is truly our Father, and that we are truly his children. We therefore are to pray to him with complete confidence just as children speak to their loving Father."

The prayer Jesus taught his followers is an invitation to them to participate in God's kingdom. When we pray, "Your kingdom come, your will be done on earth," we are praying that the father's will be done through us. Forgiveness is at the heart of the father's will: forgiveness for us and forgiveness from us. Forgiveness is a gift from God to us; it is also God's expectation of us: "Forgive us our sins, *as we* forgive those who sin against us." Forgiving and being forgiven are like the two sides of a coin. Refuse to forgive and you will not be forgiven.

Some time ago a friend sent me a copy of a Canadian newspaper that reported on the funeral of hockey player Dan Snyder. Snyder was killed when the Ferrari driven by former college hockey great and NHL rookie of the year, Dany Heatley, went out of control and crashed. Heatley and Snyder were teammates and roommates. Heatley, twenty-two, was charged with vehicular homicide in the crash.

The funeral for Dan Snyder was held at the Elmira Mennonite Church in Elmira, Canada, a little town near Kitchener and Waterloo. Outside the church Dan Snyder's family released this statement: "We are all human beings and we know that humans make mistakes. We want you to know that we do not lay blame on Dany Heatley for the accident that took our son from us. Forgiveness is also a part of being human and we know there is nothing to gain from harboring resentment or anger toward others. We are here to support (Dany) Heatley through this difficult time and know that he too is hurting so much."

I know nothing more about the Snyder family, but it is clear that it is a family that will heal. Forgiveness heals. The Snyder family understands and has embraced the prayer Jesus taught to his followers.

Every day we are in need of forgiveness, in need of the second chance that forgiveness gives. Every day we also are presented opportunities to forgive people we know. Forgiveness is a giving up of resentment and offering to the person who harmed us a new start. Forgiveness is a gift we offer to others, allowing them a second chance in life, a chance to start over after their behavior has hurt us. It's the way God is with us; it is the way God expects us to be with others.[1]

*"Forgive us our sins as we forgive those who sin against us."*
There is not the slightest suggestion that we are offered forgiveness on any other terms.

# { seventy times seven }

*Then Peter came and said to him, "Lord, if another member of the church sins against me, how often should I forgive? As many as seven times?" Jesus said to him, "Not seven times, but, I tell you, seventy-seven times."*
—*Matthew 18:21-22*

My first counseling session took place under the streetlight in front of Earl Pierce's home when we were eleven years old. Earl didn't go to Sunday school and I did, so it was appropriate that he directed his theological question to me. "Isn't it a rule," Earl asked, "that if you pray for God to forgive you twelve hours before you die he has to let you go to heaven?"

Lest you figure the twelve-hour number was arbitrary, let me tell you that Earl was hoping that if he merely prayed twice a day, he was home free no matter what he did in between prayers. Earl was looking for a loophole in the kingdom. Like the apostle Peter, Earl was trying to quantify grace, trying to do as little as possible for maximum benefit. Grace doesn't work that way.

Peter knew that forgiveness was not a one-time thing, and he was feeling quite generous by suggesting that forgiving another seven times was more than enough. The trouble was, in trying to quantify forgiveness—and grace—he was miles away from where Jesus was.

You've heard it said that to err is human and to forgive is divine. It is true. True forgiveness is not a human possibility; it comes from God. We learn to forgive not by trying harder, but by giving the other person, and the situation, and ourselves over to God.

In the remarkable autobiography by Corrie ten Boom entitled, *The Hiding Place,* she tells how she, her sister, Betsy, and their father turned their home in Holland into a sanctuary for Jewish people during World War II. Many people hid with them a day or two until someone could take them out of the country to safety. Others stayed much longer. Driven by their faith in God, the ten Boom family willingly risked their lives to care for Jewish people. Inevitably, they were reported, convicted for harboring Jews, and thrown into prison where Betsy and their elderly father died.

After the war was over Corrie traveled around the world telling her story and talking about the love and forgiveness of God. One night she spoke in a church, and when she was finished she was approached by a man with a bright smile and an extended hand. She immediately recognized him as the chief guard of the concentration camp where her sister had died. "Fraulein," he said, "how grateful I am to hear that Jesus washed away my sins."

Corrie wrote that she was paralyzed as the guard approached. She could not raise her hand from her side. "Even as vengeful thoughts boiled through me, I saw the sin of them . . . and yet I could do nothing about it. I could not feel even the slightest spark of love or charity. And so I breathed this silent prayer, 'Jesus, I cannot forgive him, please give me your forgiveness.'" And in a moment she felt the power to lift her hand and shake the hand of the man who had persecuted her and her sister. She closed with this comment, "When our Lord tells us to love our enemies, he gives us, along with the command to do it, the love itself."

Forgiveness is a gift from God that goes against much of what we know in this life. Whoever says, "Don't get mad, get even," is simply reflecting the dominant cultural attitude. We cannot make ourselves forgive anyone, but we can allow God to work through us to forgive. God gives us the power not just to forgive once, but over and over again. When Peter asked Jesus if he had to forgive seven times Jesus countered by saying, "no, seventy times seven," which was his way of saying, "Stop keeping score."

Forgiveness happens when we allow God's love and forgiveness to flow through us. In this sense we begin to live the life we have with God. God forgives us continually. God forgives us before we even ask. In a relationship of love forgiveness is continual. It goes far beyond seven times or even seven times seven times. Forgiveness is nothing less than a concrete expression of love.

We often say, "forgive and forget," but the two are not necessarily linked. If someone hurts you it is possible to release them from the damage they have done, but it may be neither prudent nor possible to forget.

A man once terminated an employee who did great harm to him. The employee asked to meet with his former employer in the presence of a third party. He started the meeting by asking to be forgiven. The employer said he was willing to start the process of forgiving, knowing it was not a simple matter to quickly wave off a hurt that deep.

As soon as he indicated his willingness to forgive, the former employee said, "Okay. Now give me my job back."

The employer said, "I want to forgive you, but I don't want to work with you again."

"Then you really haven't forgiven me, " the employee said.

The third party then told the former employee, "I think you are confusing forgiveness with reconciliation. Your employer is willing to forgive you, but not to reconcile with you. Forgiveness and reconciliation are quite different. Your employer has agreed not to hold your error against you, but is not willing to re-employ you."

The former employee said, "Then what good is forgiveness?"

The third party said, "I feel sad that you don't know the answer to your own question.

When I say, "I forgive you," it doesn't mean I've changed my mind and now think you're a great person. Forgiveness is not an offer to live as if the past has never taken place. If so, forgiveness would be mere sentimentality.

Forgiveness is a loving voluntary cancellation of a debt. It is the willingness to release the erring party from the past and not to press moral charges. To say I forgive you is to begin the process of eliminating bitterness and all thoughts of revenge. It is to wish the other person well, and set them free without having to carry the burden of yesterday's sins on their shoulders.

This is the good news of God. In Jesus, God offers you and me both forgiveness and reconciliation. On the cross Jesus forgave those who arranged his death, and made possible a new way of life with God. He does not demand that we be reconciled to those who have hurt us, but asks only that we begin the process of forgiveness. As time passes, that may well lead to reconciliation.

Both Peter and my friend Earl understood that forgiveness is a powerful thing. What they didn't quite understand is that it is neither mechanical nor numerical. It only comes when we allow our lives to be shaped by the love of God. As we open ourselves to the power, love, and forgiveness of God flowing through us, we are transformed and our relationships with others are transformed.

# { even my enemies? }

*But I say to you that listen, Love your enemies, do good to those
who hate you, bless those who curse you, pray for those who abuse
you.*
    *—Luke 6:27-28*

Helen Yittri is a church secretary. One Monday morning, when
she arrived at the church parking lot, she was surprised to see a
large SUV parked near the entrance. Standing next to the car
was its owner, Chick Bolstad.

Chick greeted her almost the second she got out of her car.
"Morning Helen. When do you expect the pastor?"

"Well," Helen said slowly, sensing that something was both-
ering Chick, "I don't expect him at all today. Monday is his day
off. Tomorrow he is at a conference in Milwaukee. I expect he'll
be in sometime Wednesday morning. Can I help you?"

Chick threw his hands over his head in disgust and mut-
tered, "Not unless you plan to do the preaching in this church."
As he opened the door to his vehicle he snarled. "Isn't that just
like pastor. He shoots off his mouth, disturbs the whole congregation, and then vanishes out of town!"

With that he jumped into his vehicle and left the parking lot
with gravel flying.

Helen shook her head sadly as she watched Chick drive away.
She thought, "He just hasn't been the same man since Jimmy
was in that accident."

Jimmy is Chick's son, who was severely injured about five
years ago in a two-car accident only three hundred yards from

the Bolstad family farm. Chick and his wife Mildred heard the crash and were the first people on the scene. It was brutal. Jim, who wasn't wearing a seat belt, broke a half dozen bones, most of which healed, but not his legs. His legs were so mangled that Jim has virtually no use of either limb to this day.

After he recovered, Jim, who was a physical education major in college, switched to accounting. When he graduated he started a bookkeeping/tax service that operates out of the Bolstad farmhouse. He quickly developed a strong clientele.

If Jim has accepted his situation, his father has not. Chick lives with the accident every hour of every day. He has neither forgiven nor forgotten. He lives with a rage directed at the driver of the other car, Horace Elgar, an insurance man who everyone calls Slim.

On that particular Monday Chick was mad. He was mad at the pastor, but couldn't find him to let him know. As he was driving home it struck him, why not find another pastor? Immediately he thought of retired pastor Knute Lee, who could be found around 10:00 most mornings drinking coffee at Little Oslo restaurant. He did a quick U-turn, drove downtown, and ended up parking almost in front of Little Oslo. As he got out of his car he saw Knute Lee walking down the sidewalk, heading in his direction.

"Pastor," Chick said standing in the middle of the sidewalk, "I'd like to buy you a cup of coffee, and I'd like your opinion on a subject of great importance to me."

"Chick," the pastor said smiling, "throw in a donut and you've got a partner. Any day you are buying coffee is a good day."

It didn't take Chick long to get to his concern. "I feel like Pastor David was attacking me in church yesterday. I know he didn't mention me by name, but he knows my situation. He knows how Slim ruined my life, and he stands in front of the entire congregation and tells people how they ought to deal with a man like Slim."

Knute looked puzzled. "Yesterday's sermon . . . it was on Jonah, wasn't it?"

"It was."

"There were so many things David said yesterday," Knute replied. "Help me remember some of the parts that struck you."

"Well, there was a part about the Nanovites."

"Ninovites," Knute said quietly.

"Whatever. They were enemies of the Jews, evil people, and Jonah had spotted them for who they were: people who could not be trusted. They had burned the villages of the Jews and taken their property. And Jonah was angry because God forgave them, gave them a second chance. So tell me, do you think that Jonah should be forced to forgive people who had killed his own kin?"

Knute quietly shook his head. "No," he said. "Jonah should not be forced to forgive anyone."

"That's what I say. You know where Pastor David is going with this, don't you?"

Knute shook his head.

"I'll tell you 'cause he said as much to me in his office. He wants me to forgive Slim Elgar for what he did to me and my family. Should I have to forgive Slim?"

Again Knute shook his head. "No one should force you to forgive Slim."

"You know what he said to me in his office? He said, 'You could do *yourself* a favor by forgiving Slim.' Have you ever heard such nonsense in your life? Do myself a favor by letting Slim off the hook? There is no way I will forgive that man. No way."

Before they parted, Knute asked Chick, "Will you be around Thursday afternoon? I'm coming out to have Jimmy work on my taxes, and we might be able to talk some more."

On Thursday, when his taxes were done, Knute and Jim moved into the Bolstad kitchen and joined Chick and his wife,

Mildred, for coffee. "Jim," Knute asked, "how often do you think about the accident? Is it on your mind every waking hour?"

"Not really," he said. "I think of it, but it doesn't haunt me, and I don't brood over how my life would be if it hadn't happened."

"How often do you think of Slim?"

Jim looked at his father. "When I'm alone, he isn't in my mind at all. Dad talks about Slim a lot, but Slim is no longer a big issue for me. I haven't said this before, but I don't hold Slim responsible for the accident. We were both going too fast. I wasn't wearing a seat belt."

"But Slim was in your lane. He hit you," Chick insisted.

"True. Slim was six to eight inches into my lane. He wasn't trying to hit me, Dad. It was an accident."

"He ruined our lives."

"Dad, why do you always say, 'our lives'? I'm the only one in a wheel chair."

"Jimmy, what happened to you happened to all of us. We are all in this together."

"And if we are all in this together what if I say, 'Enough! Let's move on.' Would you? Dad, you talk about Slim all the time. Pastor David is right. It is time to not have Slim Elgar run our lives. I gave him up several months ago."

There was a long silence. Then Knute spoke. "The other day Chick asked me if anyone should make Jonah forgive the people that burned his country's villages and stole their property. The answer is no. No one can force someone to forgive. Forgiveness is a free choice. What made Jonah mad was that God forgave his enemies. In his heart, Jonah knew that forgiveness is the way of God, and so do you Chick. And because it is the way of God it should be the way of God's people. And we need to remember that just because we see someone as our enemy doesn't make them God's enemy.

"Jesus told his followers to love their enemies. As long as we hate—hate with a red hot hate—those we hate control our lives. There is both freedom and the promise of a new future in forgiveness, freedom, and promise for us, and for those who have hurt us."

Mildred spoke. "Jim and I are ready to move on, Chick, but you are stuck, full of poison. You have to get rid of it."

"It sounds as if you have been spending time with Pastor David."

"Dad, Pastor David has been great to Mom and me. He had us both memorize a passage in Luke. 'If you love those who love you, what credit is that to you? For even sinners love those who love them. But love your enemies, and do good . . . and your reward will be great.'"

Here Mildred's voice joined him, "and you will be children of the Most High, for he is kind to the ungrateful and the wicked."

Mildred concluded, "I love that part. I want to be a 'child of the Most High.' Jimmy and I pray together each morning, and each morning we ask God to take care of Slim. He is no longer our responsibility."

"And Dad, we pray for you. You are a great dad. I just know you'll be even better if you can turn Slim over to God."

Chick looked at his family. "I'm not sure where you are. All I know is that I'm not ready to give him up or turn him over."

Mildred put her hand on the arm of her husband. "We'll wait for you. When you are ready you'll join us. I've known you for forty years, and you have always been a person who has wanted to do the right thing, and forgiving Slim is not only the right thing, it is the Godly thing."

# { the forgiving father }

*"But the father said to his slaves, 'Quickly bring out a robe—the best one—and put it on him; put a ring on his finger, and sandals on his feet. And get the fatted calf and kill it, and let us eat and celebrate; for this son of mine was dead and is alive again; he was lost and is found!'"*
—*Luke 15:22-24*

The critics of Jesus came from the "Birds of a Feather School." If Jesus hangs out with bad folks he must be one of them. He responded to their grumbling by telling three parables—each about the joy of finding the lost. One of the stories, perhaps his greatest, most people call, "The Prodigal Son." Though the younger or prodigal son has an important part in the story, the parable is clearly not about him—it is about the Father, the waiting or loving Father.

This younger son approached his father and made a strange request. What he said was, "Give me my inheritance now." I don't know how that would play in your family, but it would be an insult in mine. It was an even bigger insult in Middle Eastern culture. His request was tantamount to saying he wished his father was dead.

Yet the father granted the outlandish request, and soon the son headed for a "far country," a place "far" removed from his Jewish culture and tradition. He quickly squandered on loose living what it had taken his family generations to save. Once broke he was reduced to working for a pig farmer, an unthinkable job for a Jewish man.

Finally, he came to his senses realizing that even his father's servants had a better life. He decided to go home and beg for a job. He had forfeited his right as a partner on the farm—after all, he had lost a third of the family fortune. Perhaps he could talk his father into letting him be a hired hand. He rehearsed his speech all the way home.

When he was within sight of his house his father saw him coming, ran, and embraced him. The young man gave his rehearsed speech, "Father, I have sinned against heaven and before you, I am no longer worthy to be called your son." The father said nothing, rather called for his servants to bring a clean robe, fresh shoes, and a signet ring. "And while you are at it," he shouted, "kill the prized calf and hire a band. We are going to have a party. My son was dead and is alive again; he was lost and is found." And the party began. The father welcomed his son not because he witnessed deep remorse, but because he was thrilled to have him home.

When the older son came in from the fields he heard the sounds of a party coming from his father's house. A servant informed him that his younger brother had returned home and his father was celebrating. This meant that the younger son who had already spent his own inheritance was now receiving a portion of the inheritance of his older brother.

The older brother was furious and refused to join in his father's celebration. The younger son had embarrassed the father in private, now the older son embarrassed him in public.

When it was obvious that the older son wasn't coming in, the father went outside to find him. When they began to talk the older son refused to acknowledge the younger as his brother, referring to him as "this son of yours." He then claimed that he had never disobeyed his father, but he was doing something worse, he was shaming him in his own home, in front of his neighbors and friends. Children in that culture do not boycott their father's celebrations.

The older son attempts to make his father choose between him and his brother, but the father refuses. In the New Testament there are two words for son. One, *huios,* means just that, "son." The second, *teknon,* is a more tender address, and means, "beloved son." The father in the story, who is surely our Father God, says, "You, my beloved son, are always with me."

God will not choose between his children. He loves both those who live in the world's pig pens, who waste their inheritance, and the stay-at-home responsible types whose pompous ways often are more irritating than those who do mischief. God has a special word for all of his children. To the child who has wandered, that word is: "Welcome home. You belong to me." To the child who takes care of business and thinks that the father ought to love him more the word is: "You are always with me, and all that is mine is yours. Never forget that you are my beloved."

Why did Jesus spend so much time with those on the fringe, those with bad reputations? Because he was imitating the Father's way. Here is what is so amazing: God looks at and loves all his children regardless of their behavior, and has a special blessing for each. Isn't that good news?

# { the rest of the story }

*Then Jesus said, "Father, forgive them; for they do not know what they are doing."*
  —Luke 23:34

I frequently am asked questions that leave me speechless. For example, one viewer of our TV program called to ask whether Chick Bolstad (a character in a story I told on TV) ever forgave the man he detested (See "Even My Enemies?"). Another person wanted to know what happened to the two brothers in the parable of the prodigal son. "Did the younger one ever turn his life around?" I was asked. When I confessed that I had never thought about a new ending to the story the person said, "Maybe Paul Harvey knows the rest of the story."

Have you ever wondered about "the rest of the story"? Have you wondered what happened to Jonah? Did he finally do what God asked him to do? In the lives of Chick, Jonah, or the two brothers, did forgiveness change them? Will forgiveness change me? Is there any evidence that people actually live the way of forgiveness?

Some of the greatest literature in the world has struggled with this question. Victor Hugo's 750-page novel, *Les Misérables*, is a classic example of the literature of forgiveness. About seventy pages into the book Hugo sets up *the rest of the story* with a great and unexpected act of forgiveness.

Jean Valjean, the novel's principle protagonist, had been released from prison after serving nineteen years for breaking a pane of glass in a bakery and stealing a loaf of bread for his widowed sister and her seven starving children. Once released from prison he was turned away wherever he sought food or work because of his yellow passport, which identified him as a criminal.

Finally, someone directed him to the home of the bishop, though he did not identify it as the bishop's house. Valjean knocked on the door and was invited by the bishop to come in. He looked hard and tough, knapsack on his back, stick in his hand, and a fierce look in his eyes. The housekeeper and the bishop's sister were terrified.

Without waiting for the bishop to speak, the convict said in a loud voice: "I am Jean Valjean. I am a convict. I have been nineteen years in the galleys. Four days ago I was set free . . . it is the same each night. . . . I go to an inn and they send me away because of my yellow passport. . . . I look for a job and they turn their backs. Finally someone sent me here. What is this, an inn? I can pay. I have money. I am very tired, and I am hungry. Can I stay?"

The bishop turned to his housekeeper and said gently, "Put on another plate."

"Stop," the convict said. "You need to see my yellow passport. Read it. People think I am dangerous; they turn me away. Is this an inn? Can you give me something to eat and a place to sleep? Do you have a stable?"

The bishop spoke to his housekeeper again, "Put some sheets on the bed in the alcove."

At the bishop's insistence the housekeeper set the table with his finest, the silver plates and the silver candlesticks. Valjean ate greedily, and then, exhausted, went to bed and fell asleep on top of the sheets, fully dressed. In the night he got up, put the silver plates in his knapsack, jumped the wall, and fled.

In the morning the theft was discovered by the housekeeper who angrily informed the bishop. As they were talking three policemen arrived holding a captured Jean Valjean. As one of the gendarmes approached the bishop addressed the convict.

"Ah, there you are! I am glad to see you. But I gave you the candlesticks also, which are silver like the rest, and would bring two hundred francs. Why did you not take them along with your plates?"

Jean Valjean was taken aback, and the brigadier was struck nearly dumb. "Then what the man said was true? We met him. He was like a man who was running away, and we arrested him in order to see. He had this silver."

"And he told you," the bishop said with a smile, "that it had been given him by a good old priest with whom he had passed the night. And you brought him back here? It is all a mistake."

"Then we can let him go," said the brigadier.

And they did. Once the police left, the bishop spoke to the ex-convict. "Take the candlesticks as well. And when you come next time you can enter through the front door, rather than the garden. It is closed only with a latch, day or night . . . never forget that you have promised me to use this silver to become an honest man."

Jean Valjean, who had no recollection of any promise, stood confounded. The bishop spoke again, "Jean Valjean, my brother, you no longer belong to evil, but to good. It is your soul that I am buying for you. I withdraw it from dark thoughts and from the spirit of perdition and I give it to God."

The remaining 644 pages of the novel are *the rest of the story.* They tell the tale of Jean Valjean's rebirth through the bishop's free gift of forgiveness. He lived like a new man.

We would not have been surprised if the bishop and the police threw Jean Valjean back in jail. We are not surprised by punishment, whether it is fair or unfair. What surprises us is mercy. What catches us off guard is grace. In the sacred story of Jesus, where grace and mercy abound, we are constantly being surprised.

In Mel Gibson's movie, *The Passion of the Christ,* there is a memorable scene where a group of men push a terrified woman toward Jesus. There are no spoken words, but our memories go to the eighth chapter of John where the religious leaders say, "This woman was caught in the act of adultery. According to the law of Moses we are to stone her. What do you say?" Jesus kneels and writes in the sand, and says, "Let the one who is without sin be the first to cast a stone." One by one the men leave until the woman stands before Jesus alone. He looks to her and says, "Is there no one left to condemn you?"

She says, "No one, Lord."

He replies, "Neither do I condemn you. Go, but don't sin again."

In the movie no one speaks a word, but rocks slowly fall out of the hands of all the men.

But that isn't the end. On the cross, as Jesus is crying out to God, "Father, forgive them, they don't know what they are doing," huge stones fall from the sky near the cross. Then the camera focuses on Mary, the mother of Jesus, who opens her hands and lets her stones fall to the ground. Forgiveness is God's way, and all who want to walk with God must get rid of their stones. There is no stone-throwing in the kingdom of God.

Jesus didn't just preach forgiveness, he lived it. The words, "Father forgive them, they don't know what they are doing," are at the heart and core of the Christian gospel.

On the cross Jesus invites us into a world of forgiveness. This world of forgiveness changes our world. It challenges those of us who are prone to throwing stones, or carrying grudges, to find another way.

# questions for further reflection on forgiveness

1.  Remember a time when someone forgave you. What happened to you? What happened to the person who forgave you? How did this change your relationship with one another?

2.  Why is it important to forgive others? What happens to us when we fail to forgive people who hurt or harm us? What happens to the other person when we fail to forgive them?

3.  Discuss the difference between forgiveness and reconciliation. Share a time when forgiveness did not end with reconciliation. Share a time when forgiveness did lead to reconciliation.

4.  Is it realistic to believe that people will actually forgive their enemies? What makes it possible for us to forgive?

5.  If someone said to you, "Teach me how to forgive," what would you say? What is the first step in forgiveness? What are the succeeding steps?

# part two

---

## amazing grace

# { zacchaeus }

*Zacchaeus just stood there, a little stunned. He stammered apologetically, "Master, I give away half my income to the poor—and if I'm caught cheating, I pay four times the damages." Jesus said, "Today is salvation day in this home!"*
—Luke 19:8-9, The Message

There is a group of biblical scholars who study not only the words and themes of New Testament stories, but also their shape and form. Normally I don't find their conclusions enlightening, but as I was studying Luke's story of Zacchaeus I discovered that scholars list it as a healing story because it has the shape and form of other healing stories. Most of the stories under the healing category refer to people who are paralyzed, blind, or suffering from seizures. Not Zacchaeus. His condition is that he is rich. Can wealth be an illness?

Have you read the story of J. Paul Getty, once listed as the richest man in the world? He was totally estranged from all five of his wives and every one of his children. In the words of his biographer, "He only loved oil."

The sickness of the Kennedy family, whose star-crossed lives have captured the attention of a nation, is well known. The Kennedy family wealth was built on the illegal activities of Joseph, the father. Though it doesn't appear that his sons imitated his business ethics, they unfortunately copied his womanizing. To listen to the stories of Andrew Carnegie, the American tycoon who built thousands of libraries across the country, or John D. Rockefeller, a Baptist who built chapels and endowed seminaries, is to hear tales of deception and fraud. How many rich people have made their money at the expense of others?

Unlike most physical ailments, addiction to wealth can result in deep spiritual illness. Often wealth is gained when truth is traded for a lie. Often the accumulation of wealth causes the ravaging of the environment. Ironically, wealth often dampens the gratitude and lessens the joy of those whose lives are given over to getting it. Many who have won huge sums of money playing Powerball have learned that large sums of money always change our lives, and seldom for the good.

Zacchaeus was the Jewish head of the Roman IRS division in the gateway town of Jericho, a thriving little city. As chief tax collector, or we might say toll collector, Zacchaeus received a percentage of every dollar his workers raised. The more his workers gathered, the more he made for himself. Most taxes went to help pay the salaries of a foreign army, an army that was hated by the entire Jewish population.

Tax collectors were labeled collaborators and cheats and were despised. Chances are Zacchaeus had great wealth, but little else. The Romans despised the Jews who worked for them, and no self-respecting Jew would ever socialize with one of their own who was collecting money for the Romans. Furthermore, tax collectors were not allowed to serve as judges, could not serve as a witness in court, and synagogues would not accept their tainted money as alms. They were non-persons.

It seems that Zacchaeus, who was vertically challenged, was fascinated with Jesus. He climbed a tree to see Jesus as he and his disciples walked by. Jesus, who the gospels tell us was forever being interrupted, stopped at the tree, called the little man by name, and invited himself to dinner. "Zacchaeus," Jesus shouted, "hurry down. I must eat with you." Zacchaeus was thrilled.

Jesus had the ability to spot need from a distance, even in the midst of a crowd. He was aware of the special touch of a hemorrhaging woman, he understood the need of a weeping mother, and noticed the expressions on the faces of a paralyzed man and his friends. This time he saw a little rich man ridiculously sitting in a tree, suffering from his wealth.

The religious leaders were upset when Jesus spent time with this traitor. They were equally upset when Jesus spoke to a woman caught in the act of adultery, or when a woman of the street wiped his feet with her hair. No matter. Jesus didn't come to meet expectations, but to change them.

Bernie Siegel writes in *Love, Medicine and Miracles* that love is key to health. People who are in the midst of a loving relationship suffer fewer illnesses. He writes, "I feel that all disease is ultimately related to a lack of love or to love that is only conditional, for the exhaustion and depression of the immune system leads to physical vulnerability. I also feel that all healing is related to the ability to give and accept unconditional love."[2] Too strong? Perhaps. But we are all aware of the terrible toll that lovelessness takes. We also know that shortly after a major loss people are apt to become ill. On the other hand, we know what happens when people experience a great love. We know that love changes attitudes. Martin Luther King Jr. used to tell those who marched with him, "Those whom we wish to change, we must first love." Zacchaeus felt the love of Jesus and it healed and transformed him.

His healing from the addiction of wealth was immediate. Without any prodding from Jesus, without pressure from anyone, this man who suffered from the sickness related to his ill-begotten wealth, began the healing process. "Half my possessions I give to the poor; and if I have defrauded anyone of anything (and he probably had), I will pay back four times as much." In cases of fraud the law required a two-to-one restitution. Zacchaeus doubled that. And without being forced!

Saying, "Please forgive me" can be a cheap attempt to get off the hook. Those who seek a full recovery from the illness of alcoholism using the twelve-step method must finally make a list of those their addiction has hurt and then settle the score with them. They do this not only for the sake of the wronged party, but for their own sake as well, that they may be set free and healed. Zacchaeus' act of restitution and generosity put his past behind him.

Jesus accepted Zacchaeus, and it created a desire for change. Zacchaeus longed for the simplicity and honesty of the teacher. He knew that if he wanted the peace that passes all understanding he would have to do some serious house cleaning. God does not force repentance. Having met Jesus, the desire to make our lives look more like his is motivation enough.

Many people assume that one has to be sad and mournful in order to repent. Not necessarily. In this story there is no sack cloth or ashes. Repentance for Zacchaeus was an act of pure joy. He was trading sickness for health, a life of destruction for a life with God. This is good news.

Jesus responded to Zacchaeus by saying, "Today salvation has come to this house." The word *salvation,* which we often associate only with heaven, actually means total well-being, health. Zacchaeus literally was made healthy through his encounter with Jesus the healer.

For Zacchaeus, healing began with a meal. It might begin that way for us, or it might begin with the simple awareness that nothing can separate us from the love of God. Grace is amazing.

# { caught in the act }

*Jesus straightened up and said to her, ". . . Has no one condemned you?"*
*She said, "No one, sir."*
*And Jesus said, "Neither do I condemn you. Go and from now on do not sin again."*
*—John 8:10-11*

When Shusaku Endo, the great Japanese novelist, was growing up near Tokyo, life was hard. Living in a country where less than one percent of the population was Christian, Endo, raised by a devout Christian mother, felt a constant sense of alienation. He was often bullied by classmates for his association with a Western religion.

When World War II was over Endo traveled to France as one of the first Japanese exchange students. He again experienced abuse, being called a "slanty-eyed gook." He had graduated from religious to racial persecution.

Rejected in his homeland, rejected in his spiritual home-land, Endo underwent a grave crisis of faith. Then he visited Palestine to research the life of Jesus, and while there he discovered that Jesus also knew rejection. In fact, he learned Jesus' life was defined by rejection. His neighbors laughed at him, his family questioned his sanity, his closest friends betrayed him, and the Roman and Jewish authorities traded his life for that of a terrorist. Throughout his ministry Jesus gravitated toward the poor and the rejected ones, the riffraff.

During the time he was studying Jesus in Israel, another great revelation struck Endo. He had always viewed Christianity as a religion of power and prestige. He had read about the Holy Roman Empire and the glittering Crusades, and he had admired the grand cathedrals of Europe. Now, as he studied the Bible in the land where it had been written, he realized the extent to which Jesus had been disgraced in his own country. He was the one Isaiah had written about, a man "despised and rejected by all, a man of sorrow and familiar with suffering" (Isaiah 53:3). Jesus, Endo suddenly realized, was one who could certainly understand the rejection that he was experiencing.

Through his study of Jesus, Endo made still another discovery, the most important one of all; God is defined not as much by holiness as by mercy. Jewish religion spoke primarily of God as the Almighty One, the One totally different from us. This God was the God of righteousness, the God of law, the God who demanded that those who worship him also be a holy people.

Jesus, without ever denying the holiness of God, demonstrated through his life that God's mercy supersedes his holiness. The mercy of Jesus, however, was frequently on a collision course with the "holiness" of the religious leaders of his day. They criticized him when he ate at the home of Zacchaeus, the collaborating tax collectors. They were irate when he encouraged children to be a part of his community, when he touched lepers, healed on the Sabbath, brought good news to the poor, and spoke to women in public. Over and over again the gospel writers declare that when he saw people in need, "he had compassion for them." The words *compassion, mercy,* and *forgiveness* describe what Jesus did and who Jesus was.

The story of the woman caught in the act of adultery, with which we closed the last chapter, features a clash between holiness and mercy. Jesus was sitting in the temple, the classic position of one who is teaching, when some Jewish religious authorities interrupted him by thrusting a woman into the circle where he was teaching. If you find it strange and upsetting that they didn't bring the man with them, you are on the same page with Jesus.

One of the men announced the charge—adultery. Someone else reminded Jesus of what the law required. The woman should be stoned. It was clear to everyone that this was a trap. It appeared Jesus was being forced to choose between law and mercy, and would offend someone regardless of his choice. Jesus, however, was a master at turning the tables on those who would trap him. He didn't answer immediately; he leaned over and wrote with his finger in the earth. Then he looked up at them and said, "Let the one among you without sin cast the first stone." We are told that the accusers all began to leave, beginning with the eldest. If only those who are perfect are allowed to criticize, if only those who are sinless are allowed to cast stones, the world would have far less judgment, and far more mercy.

Jesus looked up at the woman and said to her, "Is there no one here to condemn you?"

She answered, "No one, Master."

Jesus said, "Neither do I condemn you."

St. Paul writes, "There is no condemnation for those who are in Christ Jesus." The experience of this woman was the experience of Zacchaeus, the tax collector, and the experience of everyone who has ever called themselves, or been called, a sinner. No condemnation. In its place there is mercy, understanding, compassion, forgiveness, and grace, amazing grace.

There are many startling things about Jesus, but one stands out above everything else. He was a friend to sinners. He ate with people who were ignored by "proper society" as being dirty, dishonest, or just plain bad. In Jesus we meet the God who gives second chances to everyone who needs a second chance.

This poses a startling question for the church today. How is it that the church that was founded on the words and deeds of Jesus, friend of sinners, is almost the last place folks want to go when they see themselves as sinners? A man is arrested for embezzlement, and immediately stops going to church. A woman is arrested for shoplifting, and she no longer enters the church doors. The same thing happens when couples go through divorce, often one or the other or both leave the church. What would it take for the church to be a place where prostitutes, thieves, and notorious sinners gather?

In South Africa, retired Archbishop Desmond Tutu presided over hearings that offered pardon to murderers, torturers, rapists, and others, both blacks and whites, who had committed terrible crimes during the awful years of apartheid. The stories that Tutu and others heard were chilling, yet the black leadership of that nation decided not to retaliate, or to seek vengeance. They invited people to confess their sins and start over. It was a terrible risk, but a risk that was greatly rewarded. Healing between races began to take place. No one but a child of the church, a follower of Jesus, would have attempted it.

God is not indifferent to our moral actions. God's mercy and forgiveness are not intended to condone or excuse hurtful behavior. Forgiveness is no license for us to continue to sin. Immediately after he announced that he did not condemn the woman Jesus added, "Go, but don't sin again." Forgiveness is a part of God's plan to give second chances.

Holiness and mercy are two words that describe God and God's attitude toward us. In most cases they are partners, but when they are not, mercy always dominates. Everyone who knows themselves to be less than perfect, gives thanks for that.

# { the ten lepers }

*Jesus said, "Where not ten healed? Where are the nine? Can none be found to come back and give glory to God except this outsider?"*
—*Luke 17:17-18,* The Message

Jonathan Kozol's book, *Amazing Grace: The Lives of Children and the Conscience of a Nation,* is both exhilarating and depressing. It is a book about the children of the South Bronx, and it reads like a trip through the devastated slums of a third world nation. This is a book that reminds me just how unfair life is in this country. Kozol's vivid descriptions of the apartments, schools, hospitals, and streets in the South Bronx make it so very clear that by comparison folks like me live in palatial splendor.

Kozol does find a few sparks of hope in what some might call a God-forsaken area. The first sign of hope—Christian churches in the South Bronx:

> Saddened by the streets, I am repeatedly attracted into churches. I search them out, and although some of the pastors speak of politics and strategies of change, it is not their politics that I really seek, but their company. Many, in their conversations, cite the gospels. When I mention I am Jewish, they have often gone out of their way to draw upon Isaiah and Ezekiel and other prophets. Meeting these men and women is a stirring experience for me. They are among the most unselfish people I have ever known. Many really do see Jesus in the faces of the poorest people whom they serve.[3]

Many people in the South Bronx told Mr. Kozol that their favorite hymn is "Amazing Grace." It is not, however, verse one where we praise the God who "saved a wretch like me" that makes this hymn a favorite. Nor is it verse four with its note of eternal hope in eternal life. The verse that catches the attention of people who live in the mean streets of the South Bronx is verse three:

*Through many dangers, toils, and snares I have already come;*
*'Tis grace hath brought me safe thus far, and grace will lead me*
*home.*

I can't relate to the life of folks living in apartments where the rats are bigger than the cats, where they walk up eleven floors because the elevators haven't worked for years, where the dope dealers declare a moratorium on selling drugs in the city park only during the hour after children come home from school, and where the asthma rate is six times the national average, in large part due to an incinerator from a large Manhattan hospital that constantly spews debris into the air.

What is the connection between the folks who live in the South Bronx and the ten lepers Jesus healed? The people in the book tell how merchants in other neighborhoods panic when anyone from the South Bronx walks into their stores. These people feel like lepers.

Lepers in the time of Jesus were required by Jewish religious law to keep a distance from non-lepers. They wore tattered clothing, rang a bell to warn people of there presence, and were forced to shout, "Unclean! Unclean!" whenever the "clean" were about. Some lepers had a very dangerous form of leprosy, what today is called Hansen's disease, while others had a very mild skin irritation. It was all seen as unclean; all were separated from society and shunned by healthy people.

In the Luke 17 story, ten lepers approach Jesus and call out for mercy. He tells them, "Go show yourselves to the priests."

Only the priest could pronounce them clean, and thus enable them to return to their jobs, homes, and synagogue.

As the ten lepers walked toward the synagogue they were healed. Nine of them continued on their way to see the priest. One of them, however, returned praising God, falling on his face before Jesus, and thanking him. He was a Samaritan, and in Jewish society, a two-time loser. He was a despised Samaritan and a leper. This man knew what it was like to be excluded, outcast, shunned.

Jesus said, "Were not ten cleansed? Where are the nine? Was no one found to return and give praise to God except this foreigner?" And Jesus said to him, "Rise and go your way; your faith has made you well." The word "well" can be, and should be, translated "saved." "Your faith has saved you."

In defense of the nine who did not return to Jesus, they were only doing as they were told. Jesus had said, "Show yourselves to the priests," and they did. Nine behaved like good lepers, good Jews. The Samaritan acted like a man in love.

People who fall in love with God do crazy things. They praise God even when they are sick. They sing "Amazing Grace" living in the South Bronx. They give money to people who can never repay them. They go through life with an anthem on their lips and an alleluia in their hearts, even when they are sick.

When it comes to God, many of us have learned how to be obedient, but few of us, it seems, have fallen in love. Love has a kind of craziness about it. Love doesn't care about the rules. Love cares about the beloved. The first sign of such love is genuine, deep, overflowing gratitude.

Our communion liturgy is called "The Great Thanksgiving," or "The Eucharist," which is the Latin word for thanksgiving. It is a small, simple meal that is intended to fill grateful hearts. Only those who know that life is a gift get much out of this meal. We begin our communion service with the words, "Lift up your hearts." We respond by singing, "We lift them to the

Lord." Like the tenth leper, you and I are invited to fall in love with God, to take inventory of our gifts, and then to lift up our hearts out of the dreary, depressing world we live in, and receive God's greatest gift, himself, through bread and wine.

# { the god of second chances }

*"Do not be alarmed; you are looking for Jesus of Nazareth, who was crucified. He has been raised; he is not here. Look, there is the place they laid him."*
—Mark 16:6

Sometime ago, the following ad appeared in an Atlanta newspaper: "Single Black Female seeks male companionship; ethnicity unimportant. I'm a very good looking girl who loves to play. I love long walks in the woods, riding in your pickup truck, hunting, camping, fishing trips and cozy winter nights lying by the fire. Candlelight dinners will have me eating out of your hand. Rub me the right way and watch me respond. I'll be at the front door when you get home from work wearing only what nature gave me. Call 437-2416, and ask for Daisy." More than one hundred fifty men found themselves talking to the Humane Society about an eight week old Black Labrador puppy. Things are not always what they appear to be.

Things were not as they appeared on that first Easter. It appeared that the establishment had won. It appeared that the government and the church had effectively silenced the teacher from Galilee who just a few days earlier had been cheered by huge crowds. His popularity irritated the Romans and threatened the Jewish leaders who, incidentally, didn't much care for each other. But exercising the maxim that the enemy of my enemy is my friend, they worked together to crucify the man who had once mesmerized crowds. Jesus was hung on a cross in the blazing Jerusalem sun until he stopped breathing. The score-board appeared to read: High Priests and Romans 1, Jesus 0.

Except things aren't always what they appear to be.

Easter Sunday, when Mary Magdalene went to visit the tomb, she found it empty. When Peter and a buddy sprinted to the tomb, they too found it empty. Then, sometime later, Mary talked to a man she believed to be the gardener, and discovered that it was Jesus. He was not dead. He was living. They had not killed him. They had not silenced him. They had not stopped his movement. Things are not always what they appear to be.

The night Jesus was arrested, Peter, who had boldly declared that he would stand by Jesus even in the face of death, denied knowing Jesus three times. When it finally dawned on Peter what he had done he went out and wept bitterly. He was con-vinced that he had ruined the best thing he had ever known, the friendship of Jesus. There was no hope that he would ever walk with his teacher and friend again.

But things are not always what they appear to be. In Jesus we meet the God of second chances. After the resurrection, Jesus asked Peter three times, "Peter do you love me?" Three times Peter said, "Yes, Lord, you know that I love you," and Jesus said, "Feed my sheep." Peter was restored as a disciple and a friend. Homecomings, even for those who betray him, are his specialty.

A few years ago, I experienced heart by-pass surgery and treatment for prostate cancer within a thirty-day period. More than once I repeated Gandhi's statement: *I know the Lord doesn't give you more than you can handle. I just wish he didn't have so much confidence in me.*

One friend suggested that I was a two-time loser. I see it dif-ferently. Unlike countless others, including my father who died shortly after he had by-pass surgery, I have a second chance in life. Things are not always what they appear to be.

One of the most tender moments in the Easter story is when Jesus called Mary by name. No lectures on resurrection. No sermon; just her name. Mary! All the beautiful sounds in a single word. The Easter story announces that the one who conquered death knows each of us intimately, and calls us by name. This is a story of grace. Amazing grace.

God blesses us with abundance, but he expects us to share our bounty. "From everyone to whom much has been given, much will be required." (Luke 12:48) God treats us as his beloved, but he has no patience with us when we treat one another as trash. To the self-satisfied of his own time who gave no thought to the needs of others, Jesus declared, "Woe to you who are rich. . . . Woe to you who are full. . . . Woe to you who are laughing." Today he might say, "Woe to those who have been graced with wealth who pay themselves huge bonuses while cutting the wages of their poorest employees. Woe to those who feather their own nest at the expense of another's pension or health plan." It is all legal, you say? God is not impressed with our legalities and says to us, "Just as you did it to one of the least of these who are members of my family, you did it to me" (Matthew 25:40).

In 1748, a slave ship named *The Greyhound* was caught in a tremendous storm in the North Atlantic. *The Greyhound* was captained by a twenty-three-year-old named John Newton, who had been at sea since he was eleven. John was tough and he was vile. Sailors were not noted for their refinement, but John had a reputation for profanity, coarseness, and debauchery that shocked most of the sailors.

It appeared that Captain John would live out his days as a very successful and wealthy slave trader, but things are not always what they appear to be. He had totally rejected the Christian faith taught to him by his mother. He told everyone who knew him that Christianity was pure garbage. On the eleventh day of the storm, however, when all seemed lost, he suddenly cried out in words he had once learned from his mother, "Lord, have mercy on me." Soon the storm died down, and the ship and its men were saved. Later, reflecting on the words that had come unplanned from his mouth, he realized that God had been with him; God had saved him.

Slowly John changed his life. He began reading scripture and studying ancient languages. Finally, he abandoned the slave trade and retired to his native England where he was ordained a pastor.

One night, some twenty years after his second chance, John Newton wrote a poem based on his experiences at sea. It began with those beloved words, "Amazing Grace, how sweet the sound, that saved a wretch like me, I once was lost but now I'm found, was blind but now I see." The poem remembered his many dangers, toils, and snares, but most of all it recalled his amazing experience of grace.

God's grace that has provided second chances to countless people can do the same for each of us. Grace can transform our lives not only now, but for eternity. For many in our secular world, it appears that at death there is nothing more, but things are not always what they appear to be. There is life beyond death. It is God's gift to us, a gift that lives on because, as John Newton put it, "When we've been there ten thousand years, bright shining as the sun, we've no less days to sing God's praise than when we first begun."

# questions for further reflection on amazing grace

1. Define or describe grace. What are the qualities of grace?

2. "The Rest of the Story" tells how a man's life was changed by an act of forgiveness (Jean Valjean). What change has forgiveness made in your life or the lives of people you know? Tell of someone who has received a second chance in life.

3. A university professor has said that students who receive a full-ride scholarship are more likely to complain about the school and less likely ten years later to feel a commitment to it than those who paid their own way. Do you think this is true? If yes, why do you think it is true? And what does it have to do with grace?

4. Describe a grace moment in your life. What happened? What constitutes a grace moment?

part three
_____

following jesus

# { god's long-range plan }

*Watch what God does, and then you do it, like children who
learn proper behavior from their parents. Mostly what God does
is love you.*
　　*—Ephesians 5:1,* The Message

On the far western edge of present-day Turkey lies the ancient
city of Ephesus. Two thousand years ago, during the time of St.
Paul, it was a seaport and the capital of the Roman province of
Asia. Today it is an unoccupied city, and due to the deposit of
silt, is located 6.2 miles inland.

Ephesus is one of the crown jewels of archeology. Tourists by
the thousands flock there daily to walk the ancient marble streets,
to view the uncovered stadium, to gaze at the baths, the frag-
ments of the Temple of Artemis, the library of Celsus, and the
relief of the goddess Nike. A visit isn't complete without viewing
the outdoor theater that once held twenty-five thousand specta-
tors and was constructed so that a human voice from the stage
could be heard in every seat without electronic amplification.

It is in this city that St. Paul spent two years of his life teaching and forming a worshiping community. It was to the people
in this city that he wrote the letter we call "Ephesians." This letter was not written only to the Christians in Ephesus. It is clear
that it was a circular letter, intended to be passed from one city
to another throughout the region. Unlike his letter to the Philip-
pians, there are no personal greetings to old friends. Unlike his
letter to the Corinthians, there are no words addressed to local
disputes. He doesn't answer previous correspondence. This is a

general letter, a teaching letter, a letter intended to rehearse the basics of Christian faith. You could call it *Christianity 101*.

What we know about Paul's time in Ephesus is recorded in the nineteenth chapter of the Book of Acts. There we learn that Paul spent three months teaching a small group of people in the local synagogue. When a group in the synagogue began to openly criticize his teaching, he moved the group to another location where he stayed for two years and continued his ministry of teaching and healing.

After Paul left Ephesus, he wrote to his friends and reiterated the faith he had taught them and its practical consequences. One of the first issues he addressed was that of racism, an issue that forever rears its ugly head. In Paul's day, racial tension revolved around the relationship between Jews and Gentiles. Jews considered themselves to be God's people, and they considered Gentiles to be outside the community of God's people.

Paul, however, declared that in Christ it was no longer so: "In Christ Jesus you who once were far off have been brought near. . . . For he is our peace . . . [Jesus] has made both groups into one and has broken down the dividing wall, that is, the hostility between us." He summarizes, "We are all one! You (Gentiles) are no longer strangers and aliens, but you are citizens with the saints and also members of the household of God . . ." (Ephesians 2:13ff).

In Chapter four of Ephesians, Paul declares that everyone has a unique gift. Since none of us have all the gifts, we form a community in which gifts are shared. The total is greater than the sum of its parts.

Paul makes pithy comments about many things in Ephesians; he speaks briefly about the relationship between husbands and wives, between parents and children, between employers and employees, and reminds us that in all our relationships we are to be "imitators of God" who, therefore, "live in love."

Paul cares about the character of Christian people. Character, he believes, consists of telling the truth, curbing our anger, earning our living by honest work, controlling our language, staying clear of sexual immorality. The biggest problem is that we often cease to think for ourselves and go along with the crowd, "the empty-headed, mindless crowd."

While Paul believed that character was formed in community, the predominant teaching of our time seems to be that moral character exists independently in the self. We all have it and it grows on its own. All that needs to be done is to call it out. It is as if we were given moral muscles at birth and that the task of the teachers of morality—in families, schools, or elsewhere—is to get us to exercise them.

A few years ago Values Clarification was in vogue. We didn't teach values. Far be it from anyone to tell anyone else what they should do or believe. We just clarified *our* values, as if all moral behavior was of equal value. We no longer use Values Clarification in name, but, in fact, it continues to exert an influence in how we think about values. Paul, as noted above, however, believed that values and character are shaped in moral communities. That is to say that values and character are not self-generated, they are formed in homes, in extended families, among friends, and in churches. Underneath moral actions are moral convictions and core beliefs.

James Davison Hunter, in a book titled, *The Death of Character*, writes:

> We say we want a renewal of character in our day but we don't really know what we ask for. To have a renewal of character is to have a renewal of a creedal order that constrains, limits, binds, obligates and compels. This price is too high for us to pay. We want character but without unyielding conviction; we want strong morality but without the emotional burden of guilt or shame; we want virtue but without particular moral justifications that offend; we want good without having to name evil. We want decency without the authority to insist

upon it; we want moral community without any limitation to personal freedom. In short, we want what we cannot possibly have on the terms that we want it.[4]

Paul does not believe that moral values and character simply exist in each of us. Our values and character are a result of the community we live in and the core beliefs we confess as part of that community. It is the result of what we have been taught through words and actions. Paul doesn't start with what we ought to do, what we should do, he starts with what God has done. He writes:

> Watch what God does, and then you do it, like children who learn proper behavior from their parents. Mostly what God does is love you. Keep company with him and learn a life of love. Observe how Christ loved us. His love was not cautious but extravagant. He didn't love in order to get something from us but to give everything of himself to us. Love like that.
> —Ephesians 5:1-2, *The Message*

Paul always starts with what God has done, and so should we. Right in the first chapter of this remarkable letter to the Ephesians, Paul declares, "Blessed be the God and Father of our Lord Jesus Christ, who has blessed us in Christ with every spiritual blessing in the heavenly places" (Ephesians 1:3). It bears repeating: who and how we are is formed in the community of faith as a response to what God has done. That is why we need to be clear about what God has done. If we are to imitate Christ, then we have to know what it is that we are to imitate.

Paul's conviction is that: "[God] thought of everything, provided for everything we could possibly need . . . and set it all out before us in Christ, a long-range plan. . . . It's in Christ that we find out who we are and what we are living for. Long before we first heard of Christ and got our hopes up, he had his eye on us, had designs on us for glorious living" (Ephesians 1:9-10, *The Message).*

Left to ourselves we are not generous, truthful, and honest. Left to ourselves we will take care of old number one. Morality is learned through observation. It is developed in a community of character where Christ teaches us how to love, how to serve, and how to give. That is why we honor Christ. Everything centers on him; everything emanates from him.

# { sacred clowns }

*It wasn't so long ago that you were mired in that old stagnant life of sin. You let the world, which doesn't know the first thing about living, tell you how to live. You filled your lungs with polluted unbelief, and then exhaled disobedience. We all did it, all of us doing what we felt like doing, when we felt like doing it, all of us in the same boat. It's a wonder God didn't lose his temper and do away with the whole lot of us.*
—Ephesians 2:1-3, The Message

When my grandson Thomas was one, he, like all one-year-olds, was extremely self-centered. I realize it is a part of survival for little ones, but what starts as a life-saving device can grow into something else. I knew that if he was anything like his father, his aunt, or the other babies in my life, his first words would be "me" and "mine!" Martin Luther used a Latin term to describe this behavior, *Incurvatus in se*, "curved in upon oneself." The issue is sin. Sin is self-centeredness.

Professor Mike Rogness, who now teaches at Luther Seminary in St. Paul, used to give the newspaper to his confirmation class and have them find articles about self-centeredness. It was easy. Be it the front page, the business section, the sports page, or the entertainment section, the newspaper was filled with stories of people putting themselves ahead of everyone else.

Not everyone, of course, believes that self-centeredness is wrong. People like the late Ayn Rand argue that there is a value to selfishness. She wrote a book on the ethics of selfishness, which is a long way from the ethics of Christ.

Even if we see the shortsightedness of selfishness we often are blind to our own situation. What we so easily see in others we often fail to see in ourselves. We need something or someone to hold a mirror up to us.

Tony Hillerman's novel, *Sacred Clowns,* does just that. Hillerman, a mystery writer who writes primarily about Native American people in the Southwest, draws the title of his book from a Pueblo tradition. In religious festivals and other community events, a small group of Pueblos called *Koshares* dress like clowns. In the novel they wore breechcloths and their bodies were painted zebra-striped in black and white. Their faces were daubed white with huge black smiles painted around their mouths. Their hair jutted upward in two long conical horns, each horn surmounted with a brush of what seemed to be corn shucks.

"They (the Koshare) represent humanity. Clowns. Doing everything wrong while the spirits do everything right." They pantomime to "make fun of how humans try to possess everything."[5] What they are saying is, we are all clowns. None of us live up to the standards of God. At times we lose sight of how we have failed. We are ignorant of our behavior, of our self-centeredness, of our penchant to do everything for ourselves. The task of the Sacred Clowns is to hold up a mirror to our self-centered behavior.

What will help us see ourselves as we really are? Who will hold up a mirror for us? Worship is for people who need a mirror to see themselves both as they are and as they might become in the grace of God. Worship is for people who *have sinned against God in thought, word, and deed, by what they have done, and by what they have left undone.* It is for people who *have not loved God with their whole heart; and not loved their neighbors as themselves.* In this, our Sunday confession, we announce that we are not who we would like to think we are, and we open ourselves to the God of second chances.

If you are my age, chances are good that you had to read *Silas Marner* in high school. Silas was a shriveled up old miser who had been falsely accused of stealing. He responded by becoming a recluse for fifteen years. His major joy in life was counting his gold. He loved to sit by the lamp at night and let the coins run through his fingers. Then a thief stole his gold and Silas believed he had been reduced to nothing.

Shortly after the theft, a destitute woman left her little girl sleeping in front of the fireplace in Silas's cottage. The next day the woman was found dead. When no one claimed the child the old miser raised her. It was an experience of delight, and it slowly changed him. He began to speak to his neighbors, and his cottage, once dark and drab, took on a new cheer. There was light in his eyes and a smile on his face. There was an outward focus to his life. No longer was he turned in on himself. The child gave Silas a reason to exist. Parenting became an experience of grace, an encounter with God.

Grace is always an undeserved gift of God. In Ephesians, Paul expresses his amazement that God didn't lose his temper when we mess up.

> Instead, immense in mercy and with an incredible love, he embraced us. He took our sin-dead lives and made us alive in Christ. He did all this on his own, with no help from us! Then he picked us up and set us down in highest heaven in company with Jesus, our Messiah. . . . Saving is all his idea, and all his work. All we do is trust him enough to let him do it.
>
> —Ephesians 2:4-6, *The Message*

Underline these words. Write them on your arm. Memorize them, for this is the heart of the Christian faith. It is all grace, all gift; we are saved by a gift. We can't do it ourselves, nor can we overcome our self-centeredness by ourselves. God does it for us. All we have to do is trust him. Listen to Paul again:

It's God gift from start to finish! We don't play the major role.
If we did, we'd probably go around bragging that we'd done
the whole thing! No, we neither make nor save ourselves.
God does both the making and saving.
—Ephesians 2:8-10, *The Message*

This is indeed the heart of the Christian faith and the heart
of the Reformation. Martin Luther called it "Justification by
grace through faith." Whatever you call it, just know that the
way we become right with God is trusting in what God has done
and is doing. It is a gift.

The Pueblo people are right. We are all clowns. We stumble,
fall, and mess things up each day of our lives. On the old Mary
Tyler Moore show Chuckles the Clown said his philosophy was:
"A little song, a little dance, a little seltzer down your pants." My
philosophy is: pratfalls every step of the way. It is based on my
clown-like experiences in life. Here is our hope; over our clown
make-up God has made a sign. It is the sign of the cross; the
sign of the free gift of God's saving, transforming love for us. We
are indeed clowns, but by grace we are transformed into Sacred
Clowns.

# { in over our heads }

*And so here I am, preaching and writing about things that are way over my head, the inexhaustible riches and generosity of Christ.*
—*Ephesians 3:7-9, The Message*

Moses was shepherding the flock of his father-in-law on Mt. Horeb when he heard a voice speaking to him out of a burning bush. It was soon clear that the voice belonged to God, who said to him, "I've selected you to go back to Egypt and tell the Pharaoh to release my people. Tell Pharaoh to let my people go."

Moses responded the way most of us do when we are asked to be a committee of one: "I'm really not up to the task." He elaborated by saying he was a nobody, that he wasn't good at public speaking, and that he really didn't understand theology. In short, he would be in over his head.

But God would have none of it. He told Moses, "All you have to do is to rely on me." Moses did, and the rest is history.

Can you image God as a director of Human Resources? All of our current rules would be broken. God appears not to be interested in credentials or resumes. For example, when God wanted a spokesperson to warn the people of God's coming judgment, he totally ignored the usual professional prophets and priests, and instead chose Amos, who described himself this way: "I am no prophet, nor a prophet's son; but I am a herdsman, and a dresser of sycamore trees . . . and the LORD said to me, 'Go, prophesy to my people Israel'" (Amos 7:14-15). Amos, too, was in over his head.

As was Jonah. If you want to send someone to warn a nation of God's displeasure, it would seem the first criteria should be to find someone who wants the job. Not God! He sent Jonah to warn the people of Nineveh that they had to change their behavior, even though Jonah clearly did not want to do it.

When Jesus was looking for disciples to carry out his work and to teach people about his way, he ignored people with education and chose illiterate fishermen to be his spokesmen. They were indeed in well over their heads.

And then there was Paul, God's missionary to the Gentiles. Paul's resume included persecuting the early Christians. Yet God chose him to take the message that he had resisted and tried to stamp out to people who had never heard it before. Was he qualified? The answer is that he was no more qualified than Moses, Amos, and the disciples. But though he wasn't particularly qualified or experienced, he was called. In his own words:

> When it came to presenting the Message to people who had no background in God's way, I was the least qualified of any of the available Christians. God saw to it that I was equipped, but you can be sure that it had nothing to do with my natural abilities. And so here I am, preaching and writing about things that are way over my head, the inexhaustible riches and generosity of Christ.
> —Ephesians 3:7-9, *The Message*

This pattern of divine behavior goes on long after the Bible is completed. Few would disagree about the great impact that Francis of Assisi made all over Europe. What were his credentials? Only that he had failed as a warrior and hadn't done well working for his father in the cloth business. Augustine, the greatest theologian of the early church, was a playboy devoted to the pursuit of women. And yet they were called by the God of second chances and they accepted the call and the grace that went with it.

And so it has always been, and, I suspect, always will be. It appears that most pastors, lay professionals, and volunteers in the ministries of the church have felt that they were in over their heads in answering the call of God.

We see a theme here. God is forever calling people to tasks that appear to be beyond their skills. Rather than call the "qualified," those who would tell you in an interview that they are able to handle the task with no difficulties, God calls people who appear to have few skills or abilities. Perhaps the point is this: since these unqualified folks don't have the necessary qualifications, they have to rely on the power of God to get the task done.

It is not only in the area of ministry that we often find ourselves "in over our heads." It is true for many of the most important tasks of life. Only a fool would tell you that he or she is totally ready to be married. And then there is the business of being a parent. Even books and classes in child development won't prepare us for taking care of a totally dependent human being twenty-four-hours a day. Fortunately, most of us have been home schooled in many of life's major areas. Still, when the day comes to start our new adventure, the best pastor, parent, or marriage partner throws him or herself into the hands of God and prays his or her way through one day at a time.

There is a lot of talk in church circles about discovering God's plan for our lives. I have yet to read anything in scripture about a plan. It seems just the opposite. Rather than a plan, we are given a God who leads us a step at a time, never revealing the next step. God directs us by being a guiding presence, not by giving us a map. Moses, Amos, Paul, and other disciples were asked to follow God day by day.

What is God calling you to do? Is it a task that is beyond your grasp? Is it to do a work where you are a leader or a supporter? If God is tapping on your shoulder, calling you to some challenge, how can your community of faith support you? Your first step may be to listen carefully to St. Paul who has terrific advice:

> My response is to get down on [your] knees before the Father, this magnificent Father who parcels out all heaven and earth. [Ask] him to strengthen you by his Spirit—not a brute strength but a glorious inner strength—that Christ will live in you as you open the door and invite him in. [Ask] him that with both feet planted firmly on love, you'll be able to take in with all Christians the extravagant dimensions of Christ's love. Reach out and experience the breadth! Test its length! Plumb the depths! Rise to the heights! Live full lives, full in the fullness of God. God can do anything, you know—far more than you could ever imagine or guess or request in your wildest dreams! He does it not by pushing us around but by working within us, his Spirit deeply and gently within us.
> —Ephesians 3:14-19, *The Message*

# questions for further reflection on following jesus

1. In Paul's day there was great racial tension between Jews and Gentiles. Where is racial tension experienced in your community?

2. Read Ephesians 2 and ask yourself how what Paul writes equips Christians to deal with racial problems. What is the key message of Ephesians that helps us deal with racial issues?

3. Share a time when you or a friend appeared to be "in over your head" and yet succeeded in getting the task done. What allowed you to succeed?

4. When a very difficult task is before you, how do you know whether you are being called by God to tackle it or whether you are being led by ego?

5. What is "justification by grace through faith?" Why is it important? Why is it so difficult for us to comprehend?

# part four

---

## exploring the core

# { first things first }

*One of the scribes came near and heard them disputing with one another, and seeing that he answered them well, he asked him, "Which commandment is the first of all?" Jesus answered, "The first is, 'Hear, O Israel: the Lord our God, the Lord is one; you shall love the Lord your God with all your heart, and with all your soul, and with all our mind, and with all your strength.' The second is this, 'You shall love your neighbor as yourself.' There is no other commandment greater than these."*
—*Mark 12:28-31*

The central conviction of Biblical faith is this: We are to put first things first. That is the essence of the first commandment: "You shall have no other gods." What does this mean? According to Martin Luther, it means, "We are to fear, love, and trust in God above everything else."

When asked by a scribe to list the first commandment, Jesus quoted the Shema: "Hear, O Israel: The LORD is our God, the LORD alone. You shall love the LORD your God with all your heart, and with all your soul, and with all your might" (Deuteronomy 6:4-5).

The principle is simple. Highest priorities must go first. If you wait until you have time for your highest priorities, hoping that things will work out, they won't.

An expert in time management was speaking to a group of students. He pulled out a one-gallon, wide-mouth mason jar and set it on a table in front of him. Then he produced a dozen fist-sized rocks and carefully placed them, one at a time, into the jar. When the jar was filled to the top and not another rock of that size would fit, he asked, "Is this jar full?"

Everyone in the class said, "Yes."

He reached under the table and pulled out a bucket of gravel. He then dumped the gravel slowly into the jar, pausing to shake the jar, which allowed the gravel to work itself down into the spaces between the big rocks. He then asked again, "Is this jar full?"

By this time the class was on to him and responded, "Probably not."

He smiled and pulled up a jar of sand, which he poured in the jar. The sand slid into the spaces between the gravel and the rocks.

Again he asked, "Is this jar full?

This time the class shouted, "Absolutely not!"

"Right you are," he said as he pulled up a pitcher of water and began to pour it until the jar was filled to the brim. When he finished he asked, "What did you learn from this exercise?"

One student said, "I learned that no matter how full your schedule appears, if you try really hard, you can always fit some more into it."

The class booed, and waited for the teacher's response. "What I learned," he said, "is that if you don't put the big rocks into your jar first you'll never get them in at all!"

What are the big rocks in your life? Jesus told his disciples that God is the first of the big rocks. If we get this right everything else has a chance of going right.

There is a healthy way and an unhealthy way to care for everything in this wonderful world. A little bit of wine is good for you. One of my doctor friends calls it "a cup of health." In the right amounts it is precisely that. In the wrong amounts it is anti-health.

There is an order to the universe. If we love God first, and our spouse, children, and friends next, we've got it right. Loving

God first and seeking to live God's way means we can love our wife, children, and friends in a proper and healthy way.

Putting first things first is not only the key to investing our time and energy, it is the key to investing our money. Christians have confessed that everything we have comes to us as a gift. We don't really own anything. There will be no U-Haul connected to our hearse. When John D. Rockefeller died he had more money than anyone on earth. At his death a newspaper cartoonist drew a picture that asked, "How much did John D. Rockefeller leave?" The answer, of course, was that he left it all. And that will be true for all of us.

At the core of our faith lies the conviction that all things belong to God. We are trustees, stewards of God's gifts. The land, the paper money, the stock that we "own" is held in trust. That is why giving is such an important aspect of our lives. It recognizes the true owner.

Another way of putting first things first is to confess that Jesus is Lord. He shapes my values. He determines my priorities. He does this in my personal life, as well as in my professional life. We always ask, "If Jesus is Lord, then how do I live with my family, use my time, and conduct my business?"

When we say Jesus is Lord, it means we are not. It means that we can't be. We don't have to make everything come out our way.

Saying God is first doesn't mean everything suddenly becomes easy. We don't always do the things we want to do or plan to do. Sometimes we do the very things we dislike. In these moments we go to God and ask for God's help to put first things first. We keep asking God to help us identify the big rocks, and then give us the wisdom to put them in our jars first. The key, Jesus said, is to seek first the kingdom of God and what is right, and then things will shake out.

# { the arrow always comes down }

*God's promise arrives as pure gift. That's the only way everyone can be sure to get in on it, those who keep the religious traditions and those who have never heard of them.*
—Romans 4:16, The Message

If you plan to spend any time working in the church one of the first words you ought to know is *adiaphora*. The word means: not of the essence, or no big deal. It refers to the many things that are purely a matter of taste and not worthy of a major dispute. Most fights in the church are over *adiaphora*. People fight over trivia and often ignore the big things. We fill our jars with the little rocks and the big rocks never get in.

For eight years I served as an assistant to the bishop of the then American Lutheran Church in Michigan. Our office was often asked by congregations to help settle disputes over such life-changing issues as the color of the carpet runner. One day the bishop was tired of dealing with *adiaphora* and sent me, his young assistant, to meet with a congregation where a group of people were upset because their pastor made the sign of the cross when he prayed in front of the congregation. The church council had arranged for two people to present the case for and two against the pastor making the sign of the cross.

When they finished I told them that the issue was not worthy of a major dispute in their church. "Besides," I said,

"Your dispute is not with your pastor. It is with Martin Luther, who urged all Christians to make the sign of the cross." I then read a passage from Dr. Luther told people to make the sign of the cross in the morning when they got up and at night before they went to bed to remember their baptism.

I was not trying to make light of their debate, but the issue really was adiaphora. Whether anyone makes the sign of the cross or doesn't is not critical to the life of faith. I suggested to them that we all go downtown, eat pizza together, and talk about some of the crucial things facing their congregation. About half the group accepted my invitation, people from both sides of the debate, and we had a great conversation.

What is a crucial issue? Knowing Jesus. Understanding what it means to be a disciple, to learn from and follow Jesus. Learning how we can best love our poorer brothers and sisters. Discovering how to connect with God.

Take the last one, how we make contact with God. It isn't easy. We don't see God, and when we pray most of us suffer from a form of Attention Deficit Disorder. Our minds wander continuously.

So, does that mean we just have to try harder? The key, I believe, is to rely on the words of scripture, "We are justified by faith apart from works of law." That phrase may sound confusing, a bit like lawyer talk, which it is.

In her book, *Reclaiming the "L" Word,*[6] Kelly A. Fryer tells the story of being in a seminary class during a particularly dull lecture. It was a beautiful day outside. Kelly began to look around the room and saw that her classmates were also looking around the room. Soon it became apparent that the professor knew he had lost his audience. Suddenly he slammed his notebook shut and stopped talking. Then he picked up a piece of chalk and went to the board and drew a gigantic arrow straight down.

"If you understand this," he declared, "you understand everything you need to know about what it means to be a Christian, a Christian who happens to be a Lutheran."

Then he left the room. As the whole class sat there staring at this enormous arrow pointing straight down, Kelly thought, "He thinks we are all going to hell."

The next time they gathered for class the professor began by drawing the arrow on the blackboard again.

"Here is what this means," he said. "God always comes down. There is never anything that we can do to turn that arrow around and make our way up to God. God came down in Jesus. And God still comes down in the bread and the wine, in the water and in the fellowship of believers. God always comes to us. We aren't able to go to God."

The professor was talking grace. He was talking about the unmerited love of God. He was saying what the Bible says: we have lost our way. If we are going to connect with God, God will have to make the first move. Grace, the movement of God in love toward us, is the precondition for everything we do in the life of faith.

*The arrow always comes down.* We are God's children not because our faith is strong, but because his love is strong. God desperately wants us to be a part of his family and therefore we are. Sometimes we are really good children of God, and sometimes we are rather marginal. Either way we are his children. *The arrow always comes down.* We discover and connect to God, but only because God has opened himself to us in Jesus. We follow, but only because he leads. We learn, but only because he teaches. We serve, but only because he enables. We are changed, but only because he transforms us through his Spirit.

A year after I read Kelly Fryer's book she spoke at our church. She told the story of the arrow, and reminded us that this is the essence of the faith: *the arrow always comes down.* We love because God first loved us.

Then she said, "But if I were to write that book again, I would use another diagram. It is true that the arrow always comes down, but once it comes down, it is intended to go out. At the bottom of the arrow is another arrow going to the right and to the left."

We are not intended to hold onto the gifts of God, or to savor them for ourselves. As surely as God forgives us, we are to forgive others. As surely as we are blessed, we are supposed to be a blessing. It is not enough to be loved. The next step is to be loving, to share that love. As God is merciful to us, we in turn show mercy to others. As God is generous with us, we too are to be generous people.

This downward arrow, this amazing grace—is the cornerstone of our life of faith. It is not *adiaphora*. Grace matters. The Reformation of the Church was about which way the arrow goes, and we are still fighting the same theological battles that Martin Luther fought. Some people insist that the arrow goes up. They insist we can make our way to God. We can't. ***The arrow always comes down.***

God came down in Jesus, and still comes down in the bread and the wine, in the water, and in the fellowship of believers. God always comes down.

# { a congregation of ministers }

*"Go out and train everyone you meet, far and near, in this way of life, marking them by baptism in the threefold name: Father, Son, and Holy Spirit. Then instruct them in the practice of all I have commanded you."*
—*Matthew 28:19,* The Message

At the end of his life on earth Jesus spoke to his disciples, saying, "Go into all the world and make disciples of every nation, baptizing them in the name of the Father, Son, and Holy Spirit, teaching them to obey all I have commanded you." A question that has faced the church is, "To whom was Jesus speaking?"

Many people assume those words were directed to pastors and priests. Yet for the first two hundred years after his resurrection, ministry was performed by lay people because there was no clergy. Amazingly, it was a period of unmatched church growth. During this period, churches were small and met in homes to study and worship. The leaders of these house churches were part-time. They earned their living farming, making tents, throwing pots, or doing any number of useful jobs, but many of them accepted a call to make disciples as their main work.

The first century was the right moment for the church to explode into the world. During this time, Rome ruled the whole area around the Mediterranean Sea. That wasn't the best if you were looking for freedom, but the *Pax Romana* (Peace of Rome) meant that people could travel freely without too many problems. The world had a common language, and the great Roman road systems, built to move Caesar's soldiers from one country to another quickly, made it easy for God's messengers to do the same thing.

Christians, who traveled into all the world to sell and buy various products, took time to tell everyone who would listen the story of a God who loved the world so much that he gave his son to die for them. They were storytellers who had a great story to tell. It caught on.

During this period, people passed around copies of the letters that Paul wrote to various churches, letters where he wrote about how the Holy Spirit provides gifts for ministry to everyone. In the letter to the Ephesians, for example, Paul describes how some are called to be apostles, others prophets, still others teachers or healers or administrators. A few are called to be evangelists or pastors. All of these folks were called for the same purpose, to equip ordinary Christians for the work of ministry, for building up the body of Christ. As it says in 1 Peter, it is not just ordained pastors and priests, but ordinary, everyday Christians who are a royal priesthood, a holy nation, God's own people.

In many communities, the number of believers outgrew the small homes where they had gathered to hear the story of Jesus and to break bread together. They began to build churches to accommodate the increasing numbers of people who wanted to gather for worship. The churches needed leaders, and it wasn't long before there was a professional clergy. The change took place slowly, but by the third century clergy had assumed nearly all the tasks that ordinary Christians once performed.

More importantly, it was assumed that virtually all the ministry that mattered, including evangelism and starting new churches, could be done better by professionals—such as pastors, nuns, and monks. This assumption continued virtually unquestioned for over a thousand years. Finally, in the sixteenth century, Martin Luther challenged the assumption that all important church work needed to be done by clergy. Martin was alarmed at the state of the church. Total power was in the hands of the clergy.

In a series of pamphlets, Luther challenged the system, arguing that everyone, by virtue of their baptism, is a minister. In his doctrine of the priesthood of all believers he insists that:

1. Believers are not dependent upon clergy to reach God. Jesus Christ is the personal mediator for everyone and is available to everyone.
2. Being a priest or a nun is but one favored Christian vocation. The truth is—every honest job is a place to serve God and others. The washer woman is as much a servant of God as a nun, priest, or even the Pope. There is nothing that is more important than being an honest worker, whether that work is for pay or is a part of one's volunteer life.
3. Everyone is free to interpret the Bible for themselves. They need not rely on a priest. (In order that people could read it, Luther translated the Bible from Hebrew and Greek to German and invited Gutenberg to publish it. He wrote the catechisms so that parents could teach the faith to their children.)
4. In times of need all believers can minister to one another. They need not wait for a priest to lead them. They can pray for others and care for them.

My church, Bethel Lutheran, has seven ordained pastors on its staff. Do we assume that the ministry belongs to them? Of course not. One of the goals of each pastor is to train others to be ministers. The purpose of our minister of music is not to perform all the music himself, but to involve over three hundred people in the music and worship life of the congregation. The director of education doesn't attempt to do most of the teaching. She recruits and trains others to do it. Teaching is largely a lay oriented ministry at Bethel, be it teaching children or adults. Although all pastors do some teaching, at least six of our major study groups are led by lay Christians, not staff.

We often use the term "full-time Christian service" to mean drawing a paycheck from a church. It is a complete misunderstanding of Christian "vocation." Police officers, attorneys, doctors, dentists, nurses, teachers, and road repair crews can all be involved in full-time Christian service. Those of you who take care of your children at home are more than full-time Christian servants. People in these and every other honorable vocation need to know that they are ministers, people who care for others in the name of Jesus.

In our Lutheran churches, every Sunday we have a congregation full of ministers. When we leave worship we all remind each other that service is about to begin. The pastor says: *Go in Peace, serve the Lord.* The congregation replies, *Thanks be to God.* Perhaps we ought to say something similar when we leave home in the morning, or when we depart the home of friends after a visit.

"Go into all the world and make disciples of every nation, baptizing them in the name of the Father, Son, and Holy Spirit, teaching them to obey all I have commanded you." To whom were these words directed? They were directed to all of us because in our baptism we were inducted into the ministry of Christ.

# { salvation in no other name }

*Everybody dies in Adam; everybody comes alive in Christ.*
  —*1 Corinthians 15:22,* The Message

Shortly after midnight on a Saturday night, sometime in my freshman year in college, as I lay sleeping, there was a knocking on the door of my dormitory room. Slowly, I awoke, answered the door and discovered two friends from three rooms away. One would become the sports editor of the *La Crosse Tribune,* the other a dentist, but that night they were standing in their underwear with huge grins on their face. "White-man, this is no time to be sleeping when a conference of great minds is meeting down the hall!"

"What are the great minds talking about?" I managed to ask.

"Are there many roads to God?"

There was no way I was going to be allowed to sleep, so I followed them to their room where an assortment of great minds, freshmen all, had gathered after returning from dates or from a night of consuming adult beverages. Sure enough, the topic was God, heaven and hell. Are there many roads to God or only one?

As a pre-seminary student, I was invited as an expert witness. I don't remember saying anything profound, and I can't remember if we reached any conclusions. So why tell the story?

Because we were talking about an issue that has troubled people for years, and troubles them still. How can Christians claim that Jesus is the only road to God? How can we say that Jesus is "the way, and the truth, and the life. No one comes to the Father except through [him]" (John 14:6)? How can we say with Luke in Acts 4:12, "There is salvation in no one else, for there is no other name under heaven given among mortals by which we must be saved"?

What we argued about in that dorm room over forty-five years ago is still a concern today. In short, what right do Christians have for being so exclusive? What about all of those who are Hindus, or who practice Islam? Don't we all worship the same God, but just call God by different names?

If we are going to explore the core of our faith we need to be clear—there are things of which we are certain, and there are things of which we are not certain. At the core of our faith is the certain conviction that Jesus Christ is not a savior of the world, but *the* savior. Jesus came into the world to save the whole world. He came because God loved the world, not just Christians, not just believers. "God so loved the world. . . ."

Our hope is not in religion. It is not Christianity that saves us. It is Jesus Christ. He lived for the world and he died for the whole world, which, of course, includes us. Our faith is not in the goodness of human beings; it is not in the moral power of people of goodwill. Like Anne Frank I believe that people are basically good, but like St. Paul I believe that all have sinned and fall short of the glory of God. I believe that I cannot by my own understanding or effort even believe in Jesus Christ, say nothing of saving myself. I know too much about the reality of addictive powers in my own life to think I can save myself.

I respect Buddhist illumination, and I admire Hindu unification. I have read about and even visited various utopian attempts to change the world, including several Marxist projects, but in the end I am convinced that salvation is not some vague feeling of fulfillment, not a reward for heroic effort, and not the realization of human potential. Salvation, wholeness, life with God is what God has planned for us and made possible by and through the life, death, and resurrection of Jesus. By raising Jesus from the dead, God put death to death, overcoming the last enemy in this world. Because he lives, we too shall live. This is what I know and believe.

But if I am sure of this, I am unsure about many other things. I don't know the fate of the Hindus, or the fate of Moslems, or Buddhists, or Animists or the adherents of any other religion. I don't know what happens to people who have never been told the story of Jesus, or those who have heard a false story of God and rejected it. If they rejected something false, thinking they knew what faith was about, it does not seem fair to reject them for eternity. In short, we do not judge them, God does, and one thing we are certain of is that God is fair and just. God is far more fair and just than we are, and if we would lean over backward to accommodate people in these circumstances, what will God do?

Though Jesus is my personal Lord and Savior, he is also *the* Lord and Savior, the *universal* Lord and Savior. The New Testament says that it is the intention of God that all people will be saved and come to the knowledge of the truth (1 Timothy 2:4). Will God's intention be lived out? I hope so, but I know that on this side of the grave the good and gracious will of God is not always accomplished.

There are a number of Biblical passages that make us wonder about the salvation of everyone. First Corinthians 15:22: "For as all die in Adam, so all will be made alive in Christ." Colossians 1:19-20: "For in [Christ] all the fullness of God was pleased to dwell, and through him God was pleased to reconcile to himself all things, whether on earth or in heaven, by making peace through the blood of his cross."

There are, of course, many passages that speak of judgment, of separating the sheep from the goats, passages about eternal darkness where there will be weeping and gnashing of teeth. How do we put all of this together? I don't know.

Here is what I do know. We are not the judge of the world. We are not in charge of salvation. God is, and in that we can all take comfort.

I do believe there is a judgment, though I don't have a clue how it works. I believe that the perpetrators of such heinous crimes as the killing of six million Jews will stand before the judgment of God, as will those who administered the Russian Gulags and those who have raped and murdered women all over the globe. But it is essential to say that it is God who will sort it all out. We don't make pronouncements about the will of God; instead we give thanks for the love and mercy of the Savior in whom we experience salvation.

If we are not going to spend our time judging whether others are saved or not, what shall we do? Give thanks. Sing. Pray. Love. Serve. Give.

# { the good shepherd }

*"I am the Good Shepherd. The Good Shepherd puts the sheep before himself, sacrifices himself if necessary. A hired man is not a real shepherd. The sheep mean nothing to him. . . . I am the Good Shepherd. I know my own sheep and my own sheep know me."*
—*John 10:11-14,* The Message

Not long ago, while reading a sermon by Barbara Brown Taylor, my memory was awakened to something that happened on my first trip to Israel in 1982. Our bus stopped at a small stream just outside of Jericho. The guide said, "I'm going to let you off here. If we are fortunate we'll see some things that are identical to the way things were during the time of Jesus."

We appeared to be all alone. Though we could see the road that went west to Jerusalem, the stream was enclosed by a small hill that blocked our view to the north and east. A few minutes later we had company. A man came walking down the hill and jumped into the stream, skipping from rock to rock. Right behind him came thirty to forty sheep. A few minutes later another flock about the same size led by another shepherd arrived on the scene. Five minutes later a third group led by a young girl joined in. A total of eighty to a hundred sheep ran and jumped into the water to drink.

One of the folks in our group said to the guide, "If sheep are as dumb as I've been led to believe, it should be interesting to see how they sort out these animals. I don't see any brand marks." I quickly looked and saw that he was right.

The guide smiled. "The shepherds don't look too worried, do they?"

Twenty minutes later the first shepherd was ready to go back to pasture. He walked to the top of the hill and let out a loud whistle that ended with a trill. Suddenly thirty to forty animals who were drinking leapt out of the water and ran after their leader.

Back on the bus, the guide explained that the whistle we heard was often referred to as "the shepherd's voice." He explained that, "Sheep have a reputation as being stupid, but that is because people try to herd them like cows. You can lead cows from the rear. A dog can nip at their heels and they will go whichever way they are driven. Not so sheep. They want to be led. If you drive them from the rear they panic. If you walk ahead of them they will follow.

"It is much like what you Americans do in what you call a trust walk, when you blindfold one person and have another lead. If the leader goes ahead, the person with the blindfold will generally follow at a brisk pace. If the leader pushes from the rear, however, the blindfolded person becomes afraid that they will run into something and so they put on the brakes. Sheep are like people that way."

He continued, "Unlike cows, you can mix hundreds of sheep together. They all recognize their shepherd's call, or voice, and will follow it when they are signaled. That was what Jesus was talking about. His sheep hear his voice and they follow him." We are like sheep. We like to see our leaders out ahead, not hiding in the back.

Jesus says, "The gatekeeper opens the gate to [the shepherd] and the sheep recognize his voice. . . . They follow because they are familiar with his voice. They won't follow a stranger's voice but will scatter because they aren't used to the sound of it" (John 10:3-4, *The Message*).

Sheep are looking for leaders. They want to hear the Shepherd's voice. The question is: Whose voice are they listening to?

There are many people who volunteer to play the part of the shepherd; talk radio alone has dozens of candidates. Sometimes pastors think they ought to lead the people, but our task is a bit different. We are to faithfully tell the story so that sheep can hear the authentic voice of the Good Shepherd, Jesus, the one who is out ahead of us beckoning us to follow him.

When Jesus declared himself the Good Shepherd, I suspect he knew those who heard him would think of Psalm 23; I suspect he wanted them to think of Psalm 23. The Psalm makes amazing promises:

> *The LORD is my shepherd, I shall not want.*
> *He makes me lie down in green pastures;*
> *he leads me beside still waters;*
> *he restores my soul.*
> *He leads me in right paths*
> *for his name's sake.*
> *Even though I walk through the darkest valley,*
> *I fear no evil;*
> *for you are with me;*
> *your rod and your staff—*
> *they comfort me.*
> *You prepare a table before me*
> *in the presence of my enemies;*
> *you anoint my head with oil;*
> *my cup overflows.*
> *Surely goodness and mercy shall follow me*
> *all the days of my life,*
> *and I shall dwell in the house of the LORD*
> *my whole life long.*

A few years ago, when I was wheeled into surgery for heart by-pass surgery, I was filled with the conviction that I wasn't alone. I had received hundreds of cards and phone calls from people who told me they were praying for me. I not only felt God's presence, I told my surgeon that he was going to have a good day because "a lot of people are praying for you."

Jesus concludes his words about being the Good Shepherd by saying he always has the best interest of the sheep in mind. Unlike the CEOs of the companies who recently went belly-up and took care of themselves at the expense of their employees, the Good Shepherd first cares for his sheep. "I am the good shepherd," Jesus said. "The good shepherd lays down his life for the sheep" (John 10:11).

Max DePree, the CEO of a Michigan furniture company observed that, "Leaders don't inflict pain. They bear pain." That makes Jesus the greatest of leaders. The cross tells us just how far Jesus was willing to go to bear pain on our behalf. He suffered, not so we don't have to suffer, but so that our suffering will not separate us from him.

This story invites us to do two things: think about the Good Shepherd, and then thank the Good Shepherd.

# { holy and messed up }

*I decide to do good, but I don't really do it. I decide not to do bad, but then I do it anyway.*
　　*—Romans 7:20, The Message*

There are two things that you will find whenever you delve into the life of any of those we might call saints or believers. The first is faith. Moses listened to God and led the children of Israel into the Promised Land. Jacob wrestled with God, saying, "I will not let you go until you bless me." God was so impressed with the faith and commitment of Jacob that he changed his name to Israel, and named a nation after him. God used the names of Jacob's twelve sons to name the twelve tribes of Israel. David, Israel's greatest king, wrote wonderful songs to God. Peter was the leader of Jesus' disciples and died a martyr's death.

The second thing we discover when we examine the lives of these great believers is that all committed serious sins. Moses killed a man; Jacob cheated his brother out of his birthright; David had an affair with Bathsheba and tried to cover it up by arranging the death of Bathsheba's husband; and Peter denied Jesus three times on the night before his crucifixion.

Faith and sin, aren't they opposites? Doesn't one cast out the other? How can two such opposing things coexist in the same person? Those who are skeptical of the power of faith point to the sin and say, "Faith has little bearing on life."

One of the most powerful cinematic moments I have experienced is in the baptism scene in *The Godfather*, where Michael, the new leader of the Corrleone crime family, is becoming the godfather for his sister Connie's child. The child is both his nephew and his namesake.

The scene moves back and forth from the church where the baptism is taking place to several locations throughout the city where gangland murders are in process. Michael has engineered a cold-blooded mass killing of all the rival leaders of the Five Families. While his henchmen methodically commit vicious and bloody murders that will solidify his position as the new crime boss, Michael is in the sanctuary participating in the Holy Liturgy.

After Michael renounces the devil and all of his works, the camera shows an opponent being shot while having a massage. Then it is back to the church for more of the liturgy—the pouring of the water, the mark of the cross upon the brow of the child, the confession of faith. After each scene in church the film shows another murder until all five of Michael's opponents are dead. Was there no connection between faith and life in this family?

Some would argue that this film demonstrates that Michael Corrleone simply was not a true believer. He had not allowed God to permeate his sinful heart, and his sin was a clear indication that faith had not really taken root. But can we be certain? Could it be possible that Michael, cold blooded killer that he is, is a believer?

John Wesley, the founder of the Methodist Church, a man for whom I have great admiration, believed that we can attain Christian perfection. Once we become a Christian we no longer commit sin. Christian perfection implies that we are so connected with Christ that anything contrary to love is removed.

Lutherans, however, believe and confess that all of us are, at the same time, simultaneously, sinners and saints. Luther said it in Latin: *simul justus et peccator*, simultaneously justified and sinful. The arrow only comes down. God has forgiven us. God has justified us. The guilt of our sin is removed, but the brokenness of sin continues to plague us so that even the most godly, the most virtuous among us are still sinners. Forgiven sinners, but sinners.

Does this make us all hypocrites, saying one thing and doing another? Not really. The word hypocrite comes from the stage;

it means to play a part, to pretend. To be a hypocrite means that you say things you don't really believe. You say you believe in God, but you really don't.

I believe the problem most of us face is a different one. We believe in God, we just can't and don't live up to what we believe. Even though we are saints we remain sinners. What St. Paul said of himself applies to all of us:

> What I don't understand about myself is that I decide one way, but then I act another, doing things I absolutely despise. So . . . I can't be trusted to figure out what is best for myself and then do it . . . I know the law but still can't keep it, and . . . the power of sin within me keeps sabotaging my best intentions. I obviously need help! I realize that I don't have what it takes. I can will it, but I can't *do* it. I decide to do good, but I don't *really* do it; I decide not to do bad, but then I do it anyway.
>
> —*Romans 7:15-20,* The Message

Do you recognize this in yourself? Don't you have at least one area of your life where you mess up frequently? Does this mean you are a bad person? Yes. Sometimes. What is remarkable is that you are also a good person. The frustrating thing is that you are both. Simultaneously.

Does this help you understand yourself? Does this help you cut yourself a little slack? The next time you mess up you could say to yourself, "I messed up again. No surprise there, I am both a saint and a sinner. I'm a sinner but a forgiven sinner. I'm a saint, but a screwed up saint."

Now comes the hard part. Can you do the same thing for someone else? If you really believe that people are simultaneously saints and sinners, then you aren't surprised when family members, friends, or church people do bad things. Every now and then I hear someone say, "That is not a very Christian thing to do." They are right, of course. But then we remember—people aren't 100 percent Christians. They are both Christians and non-Christians. Simultaneously.

Saints and sinners. All at the same time. Does this mean we are totally stuck? Does this mean you will never overcome that addiction, or curb that temper? No. By the power of the Spirit of God, tomorrow need not be like today. God stands beside us to help us grow. The one thing we will not overcome, however, is our sinfulness. We will always be both saint and sinner.

One of the outstanding Christian leaders of the last century was a German pastor, Dietrich Bonhoeffer. Both a scholar and a pastor, Bonhoeffer operated an underground seminary. He also wrote several books that have made a huge impact on the church and individual lives. Originally a pacifist, he finally joined a plot to assassinate Hitler after his sister asked him this question: "If a mad man is killing people in the streets, is the only option for a pastor to bury the dead? At some point doesn't he have to stop the mad man?"

The plot failed, Bonhoeffer was arrested, and transferred from one prison to another for the rest of his young life. He was bold and he was articulate. He appeared to others as the most confident of leaders. Other inmates and jailers came to him for counsel. But was he all that sure of himself?

During his incarceration he wrote this poem, which was published after the Nazis executed him.

*Who am I? They often tell me*
*I would step from my cell's confinement*
*calmly, cheerfully, firmly,*
*like a squire from his country house.*
*Who am I? They often tell me*
*I would talk to my warders*
*freely and friendly and clearly,*
*as though it were mine to command.*

*Who am I? They also tell me*
*I would bear the days of misfortune*

*equably, smilingly, proudly,*
*like one accustomed to win.*

*Am I then really all that which other men tell of?*
*Or am I only what I myself know of myself?*
*restless and longing and sick, like a bird in a cage,*
*struggling for breath, as though hands were compressing my throat,*
*yearning for colors, for flowers, for the voices of birds,*
*thirsting for words of kindness, for neighborliness,*
*trembling with anger at despotisms and petty humiliation,*
*tossing in expectation of great events,*
*powerlessly trembling for friends at an infinite distance,*
*weary and empty at praying, at thinking, at making,*
*faint, and ready to say farewell to it all?*

*Who am I? This or the other?*
*Am I one person today and tomorrow another?*
*Am I both at once? A hypocrite before others,*
*and before myself a contemptibly woebegone weakling?*
*Or is something within me still like a beaten army,*
*fleeing in disorder from victory already achieved?*

*Who am I? They mock me, these lonely questions of mine.*
*Whoever I am, Thou knowest, Oh God, I am Thine!*[7]

Who are you? Are you a good person—honest, fair, and just? Or are you a person that only a few know—full of jealousy, envious, and frequently mean-spirited? Or are you both, all at the same time, holy and messed up?

Here is what is amazing—God knows both parts of you, and loves you, the total you. You are a believer, so remain a believer. You are also a sinner, with all that implies. So be a sinner. Confess. Receive forgiveness from God and the power to fight evil. Know that you belong to God and God belongs to you.

# { transforming faith }

*Then the other disciple, the one who had gotten there first, went into the tomb, took one look at the evidence, and believed.*
—John 20:8, The Message

Early Sunday morning, before sunrise, a lonely figure walked down the road toward the Jerusalem tombs. Her name, Mary. Her hometown, Magdala, a small village on the Sea of Galilee. She had traveled south along with a handful of other women following their teacher and friend, Jesus. Mary and the other women provided for Jesus out of their own meager resources.

He was a remarkable man. Few people who encountered him were the same again. From listening to Jesus, people gained a new vision of the meaning of life. Everyone is created in God's image, he taught. Everyone. There were a lot of traveling rabbis in that day, and most of them excluded women, foreigners, and sick people. Not so with Jesus. Everyone was welcome, regardless of health, nationality, or gender. Shortly after his death one of his disciples summed it all up: "There are no longer Jews or Greeks, males or females, slaves or free. In Jesus we are all one, all equal, all special and worthy" (Galatians 3:28, *The Message*). We are not an accidental by-product of cosmic chemistry. We are not just some*thing*, we are some*one*.

A handful opposed him, deeply threatened by his message, and wanted him killed. Finally, on the day we know as Good Friday, they succeeded. He was dead by three in the afternoon and, later in the day, was placed in a borrowed tomb.

As John tells the story, Mary waited until Sunday morning to go to the tomb with special oils to anoint the body of her fallen friend. When she arrived at the tomb she was startled. In the dark she had to look closely, but it was true, the stone that had sealed the tomb was moved. Quickly she ran back to where the friends of Jesus were staying and awoke the two leaders, Peter and John, shouting: "They have taken the Lord out of the tomb and we don't know where they have laid him."

Peter and his companion sprinted to the tomb, looked inside, saw the burial cloths lying on the ground, and the head piece rolled up neatly all by itself, and were amazed. In shocked astonishment they returned home.

Mary remained outside the tomb frightened and weeping. What happened next is not totally clear, but at some point she heard her name. It was the voice of love. Only one person could say it like that. So simple. So powerful. So compassionate. *Mary.* To hear your name spoken by one you love, one you were afraid you would never see again, priceless.

Do you wonder why John in telling the story of the resurrection of Jesus spends so much time with Mary Magdalene? It is because he believes that resurrection is not just something that happened to Jesus, but something that can happen to all who believe and trust in Jesus. In a sense, Mary was the first disciple, and her life was transformed.

John wants us to know that what happened to Jesus can happen to his followers. Through the power of the Spirit, we who trust in him and believe in him share in his resurrected life. It was resurrection power that caused the church to grow from a handful of disciples to a movement that changed the Middle Eastern world in a few decades. People said, "I want what the Christians have."

People continue to experience resurrection power as they face illness, defeat, or danger. It is resurrection power that turns lives around in prisons, in ghettos, and at AA meetings. It is the power of the indwelling Spirit that holds lives together in the face of cancer, heart attacks, or tragedy.

Do you remember the story of Ashley Smith of Duluth, Georgia, a suburb of Atlanta, who was returning from a trip to a convenience store at about 2:00 A.M.? Brian Nichols was waiting for her. He was the subject of a massive manhunt. Wanted for rape and the murder of several people, he had killed the female guard who was bringing him to court. When Ashley attempted to enter her home, Nichols forced his way into her apartment, right behind her.

She was terrified. "Do you know who I am?" he asked. She didn't. When he took off his cap she suddenly recognized his picture from TV, and said, "Please don't kill me, I have a five-year-old little girl."

Ashley had a tough life. Some of her troubles seemed to just happen to her; many of them were the result of bad choices. She had been arrested several times. She had used drugs and alcohol to excess. Four years earlier, her husband was stabbed to death and died in her arms. Shortly after his death, she hit bottom. She found help during a two-month stay in a Christian clinic for drug abusers. Meanwhile, she began to live temporarily with her aunt. After rehab, she returned to church and her family felt like she was making progress. "One of these days," she told them, "you'll be proud of me."

At first the fugitive bound her with masking tape, a curtain, and an electrical cord. Later he unbound her, and they began to talk. She talked about her family and her faith. She listened to his story, starting with his time in the military. Somewhere in the midst of the discussion, Ashley told Nichols she wanted to read to him. She got a Bible and a copy of Rick Warren's *The Purpose-Driven Life*. She read to him about the purpose of life and using the talents God has given each person.

He asked her to read it again, and then asked her what she thought he should do. "I think you should turn yourself in," she said. "If you don't turn yourself in lots more people are going to get hurt." They watched TV, and when he saw himself on the news he said, "Look at me. Look at my eyes. I'm already dead."

Ashley told Nichols it was a miracle he had survived at all, and that he needed to go to prison and share the word of God with all the prisoners there. Then they had communion. Actually, it was pancakes, with real butter, but it must have seemed like communion to him because God was surely present in that meal. Finally, Nichols let Ashley leave and she called 911. He was arrested without further incident.

Brian Nichols is black. Ashley Smith is white. He is male. She is female. He is enslaved. She is free. But there is neither black nor white, male nor female, slave nor free if you are in Christ Jesus. He had done terrible things, yet she treated him like some*one*, not some*thing*. In the face of evil, Ashley pointed to her faith. She told Nichols that God would not abandon him, no matter where he ended up. She didn't argue with him, or debate with him. She simply talked with him as one who had experienced the power of transforming faith in her own life.

Ashley Smith is a work in progress. She has not arrived. She is on the way back, but quite frankly, so are we all. We just have different issues. Like Ashley and countless others, we don't have to wait until we get it all together to begin living a resurrection life, a transformed life.

Over forty years as a pastor, I have watched faith take root in lots of people. I have stood thrilled to watch what happens as people come to understand that God's Spirit empowers them to meet each day and whatever the day brings. I have been humbled at the way broken lives have been put back together and healed. I have been privileged to give this advice over and over again: "Trust that you share the resurrection power of Jesus; trust that the transforming Spirit of God is at work in you, and watch what happens."

# { the bath and the meal }

*This is what happened in baptism. When we went under the water, we left the old country of sin behind; when we came up out of the water, we entered into the new country of grace—a new life in a new land!*
  *—Romans 6:2-3, The Message*

*This Meal . . . is a spiritual meal—a love feast.*
  *—1 Corinthians 11:34, The Message*

As I look back at the days when our children were growing up it seems as if there were two defining daily events. In their early years it was the bath. At the end of a long day of playing, laughing, fighting, and crying, it was bath time. There were often two in the tub at one time, splashing, playing, or arguing over whose turn it was to use a toy. For the most part, it was a time of pure delight as they shed the layer of dirt they had accumulated from a long day of play.

The bath was not only a cleansing of the body; it was a cleansing of the soul. The child who came out of the bath was not the same child who went in. The child who came out delighted in his or her cleanliness. They could hardly stand still while their mother put fresh clean pajamas on them. Often they squealed with delight and ran through the house in a kind of joyous celebration. They were new children.

As they grew older, the bath naturally became private, more individual. Still, it was joyous. Not only did they delight in the smells of a clean body and clean hair, they delighted in the event itself. In the bath, now a shower, they sang. As far as I know, my son has never sung solo anywhere except in the shower where he sings with great happiness and joy. How can water do such great things?

As they grew older the defining event for our family became the meal. Usually this was the evening meal. We ate, told stories, remembered and shared. We laughed. We learned. We delighted in the good food that came from the loving hands of a gracious and capable cook.

There was a time when the meal was in danger. In her last year of high school, our daughter was suffering from a severe case of "senioritis." One of the symptoms of this disease is a resistance to anything connected with parents. She informed us that she no longer wanted to eat with the family, nor did she want to eat what the family ate. Her preference was to eat alone and to eat what she wanted. If we ate at 6:00 p.m., she wanted to eat at 5:00 p.m., and choose her own menu.

This resulted in her father's "This is not a motel," speech. The speech went something like this, "This is not a motel. We do not lease rooms. We are a family, and one of the things families do is gather together daily. If you prefer to eat earlier, go ahead, but at 6:00 p.m. I expect you to be at the table with your brother, your mother, and me."

And she was, frequently reluctant, but always present. After a few minutes of heavy silence she would join in the conversation. The next fall, from ten hours away at college, sometime in late October, she uttered these memorable words, "You know what I miss the most? Mealtimes." Her mother and I looked at each other and gave a silent cheer.

How can eating and drinking do such great things? The bath and the meal. Cornerstones in our family life. The bath and the meal. Cornerstones in our faith life. Both are simultaneously individual and communal.

The bath, which we call baptism, comes first. It is a public washing whether we are six months, six years or sixty years when it takes place. It is the way God makes sons and daughters. Not only is it a washing, but it is a cleansing. When we come out of the bath we are not the same as when we went in. We have been made clean. We have a new identity; we are beloved children of God.

Baptism works because God makes it work. In baptism we don't choose God, God chooses us. While we are still helpless, while we are still sinners, we are chosen and named. In baptism we are sealed with the Holy Spirit and marked with the cross of Christ forever. That cross is a mark of identity, and a mark of vocation. We are all destined to become pastors, priests, and servants of God. How can water do such great things? It isn't the water only, but God's word with the water and our trust in God's word. Water by itself is simply water, but with God's word it is life-giving water.

If Baptism is our sacrament of identity then Holy Communion is our sacrament of community. The meal is at the center of our congregational life together. The public gathering of God's people shapes itself around two events—the sermon and the meal. They are two parts of a whole. The sermon is a spoken word. Holy Communion is a visible word. The sermon proclaims the central event of the life of Christ, his death and resurrection. We announce that in Jesus Christ we have forgiveness of sins, life, and salvation. We preach Christ crucified, the cross as the only symbol of discipleship, and the resurrection as our only hope.

In the meal we see the bread, broken like his body. We see the wine, poured out like his blood. Communion is an announcement that Jesus is risen and present, sharing the power of his resurrection with us. What are the benefits of Holy Communion? In Holy Communion we receive forgiveness of sins, life, and salvation. For, as Luther taught, where there is forgiveness of sins there is also life and salvation. In communion we "taste and see that the Lord is good." Holy Communion is a visible word, a life changing word. It is a time when the family of God gathers together. We eat, tell stories, remember, and, when finished, we go in peace to serve the Lord. How can eating and drinking do such great things? It isn't just the eating and the drinking, but the words, "Given and shed for you for the forgiveness of sins," that make this meal a sacrament of Christ's healing presence.

This meal is such a powerful event that no single name embraces its entire meaning. Our Roman Catholic friends prefer the word *Eucharist,* which means thanks. It comes from that part of the liturgy were the pastor sings, "Let us give thanks to the Lord our God," and the congregation responds: "It is right to give God thanks and praise."

In our Protestant tradition, we often call this meal the Lord's Supper. It is a good name because it reminds us whose meal it is. It is not the church's supper, it is the Lord's Supper and Christ is the host. It is his meal, and since Christ is the host we welcome everyone as he did.

Perhaps in Lutheran churches the most common name for the meal we share is Holy Communion. At its core it is the same word we have for community and communication. It is easiest to simply break the word down—come and union, *union* meaning together. Thus we have a "come together." God comes together with us, and we come together as a community. God meets us in this meal. How does this happen? We don't know.

We come together as hungry people to a hungry feast. There is no head table. There are no positions of honor. We are all equal here in God's love. We all receive a small piece of bread and a small drink of wine. No one gets any more than anyone else. And as St. Mark said of the multitude that Jesus fed with five loaves and two fish, "All ate and were satisfied."

The bath and the meal—they tell us who we are. They connect us with God and with one another; they are at the heart of our life together. How can water and bread and wine do such great things? It is not just the water, the bread, and the wine, but God's word with these elements and our trust in God's word. Cherish them; they are gifts from a gracious and loving God.

# { silence is no longer an option }

*"Whether it's right in God's eyes to listen to you rather than to God, you decide. As for us, there's no question—we can't keep quiet about what we've seen and heard."*
—Acts 4:18-19, The Message

Someone you love dies far too soon, long before a full life has been lived. You are devastated. Grief nearly overwhelms you. At first you wonder how you will ever survive. How will you get through the next minutes and hours, not to mention a whole new day? But slowly (it never comes fast), you begin to rehearse the promises that you learned long ago, the promise of life beyond life, the promise of a new heaven and a new earth. You remember that your loved one is in the hands of a loving and merciful God whose son has gone to prepare a place for all of those who live in his name. It doesn't take all the pain away, but it makes it bearable. You wonder how people who don't share your hope make it, and you start a new day.

You messed up. The decision you made was dumb, and hurtful, to say nothing of wrong. What in the world were you thinking? Add to that the fact that this wasn't the first time that you blew it. You feel terrible, full of guilt. But as you get up the next day and stand in the shower feeling the water run down your back you say a simple prayer, "Father, forgive me. I have done wrong," and slowly you come to the realization that yesterday's mistakes, like the water, are cascading down the drain. You are forgiven. You have a second chance. This doesn't take you off the hook entirely. You still have to make amends and you will try. You wonder how people who don't know about forgiveness make it, and you start your new day.

Your brother and sister-in-law are coming to town this weekend, the ones with the great jobs, and the tremendous salaries and investments that they forever remind you about. You are absolutely positive that others in the family are always comparing you to them. Why haven't you succeeded like they did? Why haven't you found the pot of gold at the end of the rainbow? They complain constantly all weekend about the hours, about the pressure, about the idiotic things they have to do to please their bosses. And then you remember that vocation is one of the ways we serve a loving and merciful God. You remember that everyone is a minister, every workplace a place to serve. You think, "I am a minister. My job is not just about what I get but what I give." And you wonder how people who don't know this get through the day.

You are talking with a friend whose mother suffers from severe dementia. Your friend is frustrated and mad. Her frustration centers on the dramatic change in her mother's personality. Once a warm and gracious person, the disease has made her irritable and sarcastic. Your friend wonders how a loving God can allow such suffering in the world, and wonders how she can find God in the midst of the pain. You want to tell your friend that the loving God you know shares in her suffering. That is what the cross is all about. You want to tell your friend that she doesn't have to find God, that if she will wait God will find her, and that at this very moment God is reaching out to her, not to take away the pain but to share in it.

The world needs what we have! It needs to know that there is life beyond life prepared by a merciful and loving God. Silence is not an option. The world needs to know about the amazing gift of forgiveness. "I once was lost but now I'm found, was blind but now I see." The world needs to know that the mistakes of yesterday need not control the hours of today. There is forgiveness at the very heart of the universe. We get to start anew each day. And the world needs to know that we don't have to search for God, or try our best to please God, or climb the stairs to God. If we open our hearts God will find us and comfort us, will strengthen and heal us. The world needs to know all this. Silence is not an option.

In the Acts of the Apostles it is put more strongly. We are told that a few months after Jesus' resurrection, Peter and John healed a man in the temple area. Crowds began to gather around them. The Jewish leaders arrested them and, in order to stop the "Jesus movement" from growing, the authorities ordered them to no longer speak or teach in the name of Jesus. The disciples responded, "Whether it's right in God's eyes to listen to you rather than to God, you decide. As for us, there's no question—we can't keep quiet about what we've seen and heard" (4:18-19, *The Message*). Silence was not an option.

We who are the recipients of such great news, how can we keep quiet? That is the question Bill asked himself. Bill and his wife, Lorraine, started attending Saturday nights services because Lorraine had trouble walking and Bill could steer her and assist her more easily when there were fewer people. Bill took care of Lorraine as long as he was able, but finally felt forced to place her in an Alzheimer's unit in a nursing home.

Seven days a week, Bill visited Lorraine, read the Bible, and sang to her. Soon a couple of other residents asked if they could "listen in." He said yes, and now seven days a week, for forty-five minutes, he reads scripture, poems, and sings a few songs to Lorraine and up to twelve other people. Bill has to cut his Saturday night readings a bit short because, "I drive slower these days and it takes longer to get to church." Bill is eighty-nine, as is Lorraine. Remaining silent is not an option for him. He has a story to tell, and those who suffer from Alzheimer's disease need to hear his words of hope.

People around us need to know what we know; they need to experience what we experience. We know and experience the love that moves the universe and knows each one of us intimately. We know and experience a God who forgives and gives second chances. We know the story of a love so great that it went to the cross rather than betray the beloved, that's you and me, and everyone else. There are a lot of people hungry to hear this story. But, how will they come to know and experience this love if no one tells them? For us, silence is not an option.

# questions for further reflection on exploring the core

1.  What prevents you from putting first things first in your life? Describe a time when you failed to put first things first. Describe a time when you did put first things first.

2.  What steps can your church take to develop a strong lay ministry? What prevents this from happening?

3.  What line in Psalm 23 is the most meaningful to you? Why is it meaningful?

4.  What difference would it make if every one who attends church regularly understood that each person in church is both holy and messed up? What difference would it make if every person who does not attend church understood that church people are both holy and messed up? Which is harder for you to believe, that you are holy or that you are messed up? Why?

5.  What does the experience of receiving Holy Communion mean to you?

# part five

---

## telling the story

# { is there anything too hard for god? }

*The LORD said to Abraham, "Why did Sarah laugh, and say, 'Shall I indeed bear a child, now that I am old?' Is anything too wonderful for the LORD?"*
   *—Genesis 18:13-14*

"Most people who know me think my life has been terrific," the man told his pastor. "My business is doing well. I will make a lot of money this year, a lot of money. I've invested wisely, which is to say my future is secure. I have a good marriage and a good relationship with my two children. I've been involved in some community service. My employees and my friends think that I have been successful."

He paused, and after more than a minute the pastor said, "But . . ."

"But I'm not fulfilled. I always thought that I was put here for a purpose, a significant purpose. I'm sixty-one years old, and there aren't a lot of new opportunities knocking at my door anymore."

There was more to the conversation, but after a few minutes the pastor said, "How well do you remember the story of Abraham?" The businessman looked a little puzzled so the pastor continued.

"In a way the Old Testament begins with Abraham. Like you he was successful. He owned a lot of animals, and was a big land owner. He had a lot of servants. He had a good marriage, but something was missing. One disappointment was that he and his wife were unable to have children. Then one day he decided to pick up and leave. He took his entire family and moved hundreds and hundreds of miles away. He decided to start over. By the way, did I mention he was seventy-five years old at the time?"

The businessman nearly gasped, "I had forgotten that he was an old coot. He was called by God, right?"

"Right," the pastor said smiling. "God is the cause of a lot of change. I believe a lot of people are called, but they either ignore it or don't recognize that they are being called. Abraham did, and became the Father of the Hebrew people, and the Arab people. Three great world religions trace their history back to him, and he didn't even get started until he was seventy-five."

"What was God doing, calling some old guy like him to start things?"

That really isn't a bad question. Why did God risk everything on a seventy-five-year-old? Before we attempt to answer that question, let's catch up on the story. The opening two chapters of Genesis tell stories about the creation of the world and the creation of the first people. Chapter three tells the story of how the first people rebelled against God and tried to take charge of the world. Chapters four through six chronicle the growing wickedness of humankind and their growing alienation from God. Chapter seven tells the story of how, in response to human disobedience, God decided to cleanse the entire earth—with a flood.

Following the flood, things got bad again. This time God tried another tack. Enter Abraham and Sarah. God decided to fashion an alternative community in a world gone astray, to form a people who would live by his words. He called aged Abraham and barren Sarah to carry his command and promise into all the world. Through this couple, the God who created the world called the community of faith into being. He worked through Abraham and Sarah to reform creation.

How do we make a difference in this world? You don't have to be seventy-five to ask that question. You could be forty-two and the mother of two teenagers. Up to now you have been a stay-at-home mom, but your son will head off to college next year, and your daughter will be a junior in high school. The need for you to be home when they get out of school is still important, but no longer crucial. The question is what will you do? You are an accountant by trade, and enjoy the work, but you have long since wondered, "Is this it? Is this what I'll do the rest of my life?"

After raising children, which seemed like the most important job in the world, you are not sure you want to work with numbers all day. Your husband reminds you that you could make a lot of money, and that soon, with two kids in college, having extra money would be nice. What now?

Or, you're in college. Everyone you know is talking about interviewing for jobs. They are doing their research about what benefits the various companies offer—Medical Insurance, IRAs, and retirement packages. Retirement packages!? At twenty-four you aren't sure these are the right questions to ask. What are the right questions? Here is a start: What kind of work does the company do? What difference does this work make? If you do it and do it well, who benefits?

What is this call that Abraham accepts on behalf of his entire family? First of all, it is a call for departure, cutting loose with his past, his family, and the land where he was living. It is a call with little security. It is a call that is open-ended.

The call has an imperative: Go! The imperative is followed by six promises: 1) I will make of you a great nation; 2) I will bless you; 3) I will magnify your name; 4) I will bless those who bless you; 5) I will curse those who curse you; 6) Through you all the families of the earth will be blessed.

Abraham's call was not to go and talk about God. There is no evidence that Abraham tried to convert people into his way of thinking. Others were called to do that. Not Abraham. He wasn't called to build a church or lead a Bible study. Others were called to do those things. He was called to live among non-believers, and to practice and believe in the promise. He was called to be a blessing to them. He was to allow the kingdom of God to work through him.

Many of us live in neighborhoods where a majority of the people who live near us don't worship. Others of us live in a dorm, or an apartment building where we are among the few who gather with a believing group each week. We may not be called to convert those who do not believe as we do, but we are called to be honest. We are called to publicly live out what we believe. We are called to make a difference in the lives of others. God will work through us to bless others as he worked through Abraham.

Why did God choose old Abraham and barren Sarah? I don't know for sure, but I have an educated guess. Later, when Sarah asked the angel, "How can I have a child when I am old?" the angel answered, "Is there anything too difficult for the Lord?" If God can build a nation with a ninety-nine year old man and a woman who hadn't been able to have children, he can make anything happen. There are no excuses for us. We are to trust God like Abraham and Sarah.

Here is a reminder. Most great works are not completed in one lifetime. The promise to Abraham and Sarah that God would make of them a great nation wasn't completed in their lifetime. The great cathedral in Milan took five hundred years to build—from 1386 to 1887. Most of those who built this cathedral, or any of the great cathedrals of Europe, never lived to see their work fulfilled. Yet they were willing to expend their efforts and give their lives to a cause they would never see completed. They did it for the glory of God and for future generations.

Martin Luther King Jr. said he had been to the mountaintop. He was not allowed to see the day of equality in this country, but he knew it was coming. King David dreamed of a temple and started the process, but it wasn't built in his lifetime. Gandhi set things in motion that he never lived to see, but today India is a better country because of him.

Most of us have ancestors who came to this country not just for themselves, but for the sake of their children and grandchildren. They wanted a better chance for those who followed them. We have been blessed by their efforts. We live by faith and not by sight.

Perhaps you believe that God has called you. Sometimes God calls us to do little things. Sometimes we are called to do big things, but everything we are called to do is important. As Mother Teresa once said, though we may not all do great things, we can all do small things with great love. Answering God's call often takes risk, it moves us out of our comfort zones, challenges us to change our priorities. Almost always it will make a difference, in our own lives and in the lives of other people.

One of the things we all learned from Hurricane Katrina is that there are too many poor people in our country, too many people living in poverty without hope. There are too many who are lonely. There are too many who are ill.

We need people to work within organizations, and we need people to form new organizations. Whatever God calls us to do, we need people who will work with smiles and great joy. As Mother Teresa once said, "The poor don't need grumpy people to work with them."

We live with hope, and we share hope. We live with joy and we share joy. God still calls people. The question is, "Are people still listening?"

# { his very own blessing }

*Then [the man] said, "Let me go, for the day is breaking." But Jacob said, "I will not let you go, unless you bless me."*
*—Genesis 32:26*

Jesus lived his life with a sense of total well-being. At his baptism, before he began his public ministry, he heard these words from God: "You are my Son, the Beloved; with you I am well pleased" (Mark 1:11). He lived the rest of his life with a sense of divine favor. He lived as the beloved one. He had his father's blessing.

Some people wait their entire lives to hear their father or mother say, "I love you," or, "You mean everything to me," and it doesn't happen. If we are among the fortunate ones who have heard words of blessing and love from our human parents we live with a sense of blessing. Without a blessing we carry the world on our back. With it, the world carries us.

Some people think the greatest power lies in weapons, or force. Christians know that the power of words, the power of touch, the power of approval—human or divine—can shape lives, and determine destinies.

The story of Jacob and Esau is a story of blessing. It begins as a story of a stolen blessing, a blessing that turned sour. It ends with a real blessing, the blessing of God. The story of the stolen blessing begins with the all-too-familiar theme of sibling rivalry, the intense competition that too often exists between two brothers or sisters.

At age forty, Isaac, son of Abraham and Sarah, married the beautiful Rebekah. For twenty years they were unable to have children. When at last she became pregnant it was with twins, and the two children struggled with each other within her so much that she wondered if she had the strength to live. She spoke to God about it and God said, "Two nations are in your womb, and two peoples born of you shall be divided; the one shall be stronger than the other, the elder shall serve the younger" (Genesis 25:23).

Rebekah gave birth to two little boys. The first was red, and his body was hairy. They called him Esau, which means red. Right behind him came his brother holding onto his heel. They named him Jacob, which means to grab by the heel, or to supplant. What's in a name? In this case, a lot.

As he grew, Esau became a skillful hunter, an outdoorsman. He was his father's favorite. Jacob was a quiet man who preferred to be indoors. He was his mother's favorite.

One day while Jacob was fixing a stew, his older, wilder brother came in from the field and announced that he was famished. "Give me some of that stew," he demanded of his brother.

Jacob told him he would gladly sell his brother the stew, all he could eat, for his birthright, the right of inheritance. "What does a birthright mean if I am about to die?" Esau shouted. The deal was struck. Delayed gratification was not a way of life for Esau.

The defining event in the life of the two brothers took place a bit later, and it involved both parents. The drama began when Isaac, now blind, addressed his son Esau. "I'm an old man," he said; "I might die any day now. Do me a favor: Get your quiver of arrows and your bow and go out in the country and hunt me some game. Then fix me a hearty meal, the kind that you know I like, and bring it to me to eat so that I can give you my personal blessing before I die" (Genesis 27:2-4, *The Message)*. Esau did as he was directed.

Rebekah had overheard her husband talking and immediately sought out Jacob. "I just overheard your father talking with your brother, Esau." She then told Jacob what Isaac had commanded and shared her plot to steal the blessing for Jacob. "Go to the flock and get me two young goats . . . I'll prepare them into a hearty meal . . . Then you'll take it to your father, he'll eat and bless you before he dies." When Jacob protested that his father would be able to touch him and feel that he wasn't hairy like Esau, Rebekah unveiled the rest of her plan. Jacob would wear one of Esau's shirts so his older brother's scent would accompany him into his father's tent. She would wrap lamb skin on Jacob's hands so when blind Isaac felt him, he would believe it was Esau the hairy one, and not Jacob, his smooth-skinned younger son. The plan worked; Isaac was fooled and gave his blessing to Jacob:

> *May God give you of Heaven's dew*
> *and Earth's bounty of grain and wine.*
> *May peoples serve you*
> *and nations honor you.*
> *You will master your brothers,*
> *and your mother's sons will honor you.*
>   —*Genesis 27:28-29,* The Message

Moments after Jacob had left, Esau returned. "Who are you?" asked Isaac.

"I am your firstborn, Esau."

Isaac began to tremble and shake. "I just finished the meal, before you walked in. I blessed your brother and it is permanent."

Esau cried, "He is well-named—Jacob the heel! He has robbed me twice, taken away my birthright and now has stolen my blessing. Father, do you only have one blessing? Bless me." And Isaac did, but it was not the blessing he had intended to give his oldest son.

Jacob quickly learned that a stolen blessing does not lead to a blessed life. Wanting what was not his, practicing deception and dishonesty, not being content with who he was in his own right led Jacob to years of turmoil in his personal life and years of enmity with his brother, Esau.

Jacob, aware of Esau's anger, fled the country shortly after his father's death, locating in the country where his mother was raised. There he met and fell into love with Rachel, his uncle's daughter. He worked seven years for uncle Laban to earn Rachel's hand. The morning after his wedding he discovered that his father-in-law had switched daughters. He had spent the night with Leah, Rachel's older and plainer sister. He worked seven more years for Rachel's hand, tending to his uncle's flock. Jacob was a great herdsman, and under his watchful eye, Laban prospered.

Jacob the heel, the crafty one, worked seven more years to build his own herd, suffering frequently under his shifty uncle Laban. Finally, he pulled up stakes and fled toward home, taking all of his animals, his wives and his many sons. Just before he reached his old home his scouts brought word that Esau was riding to meet him, accompanied by four hundred armed men.

Knowing that he was no match for Esau, and fearing that his brother was preparing to take vengeance on him, Jacob secured his family and then spent the night in prayer. A *man* appeared and wrestled with Jacob all night long. When the *man* saw that he couldn't pin Jacob he deliberately threw his hip out of joint. Then the *man* said, "Let me go; it's daybreak."

But Jacob said, "I'm not letting you go until you bless me." It was time for Jacob to have his own blessing.

The *man* said, "What is your name."

"Jacob."

"Your name is no longer Jacob (the heel). From now on it's Israel (God-Wrestler); you've wrestled with God and come through."

Jacob named that place, Peniel—The Face of God—and said, "I saw God face-to-face and lived to tell the story."

At last Jacob had his own blessing. The next day he met Esau. He no longer walked like cocky Jacob, but limped like faithful Israel. The brothers reconciled.

Some of us have longed to have a blessing from a parent. Some of us have waited in vain for a blessing from either our father or our mother. It is painful. What we learn from the story of Jacob, and even more from the story of Jesus, is that each of us has been blessed by our heavenly Father. In our baptism God has declared us to be precious in his sight. God has addressed each of us, saying, "You are my beloved child. In you I am well pleased."

In addition to the blessing that God bestows on everyone, what we might call, "a general blessing," we have all received our own unique blessing, which is revealed in our own unique skills. None of us is unblessed even though we may be blind to the blessing.

God hopes that we can accept ourselves the way we are. This does not mean we should not work hard to develop new skills. It does mean that we should honestly evaluate who we are and what we have been called to do. God has a blessing for each of us. We are invited to wrestle with God until it becomes clear, then claim it and rejoice in it.

# { here comes the dreamer }

*When he told [his dream] to his father and brothers, his father reprimanded him: "What's with all this dreaming? Am I and your mother and your brothers all supposed to bow down to you?"*
—Genesis 37:10, The Message

If you are looking for a story of a well-adjusted family who exuded love and peace, you will have to look outside of the book of Genesis. All of the families in Genesis are dysfunctional, particularly the family of Jacob. Dysfunction is often the fruit of our sin. That is the bad news. Here is the good news: God loves sinners, and works in and through the lives of dysfunctional people.

When we read about the early years of Jacob, we discover that pain and disease affected the entire household. In this case the acorns did not fall far from the tree. As we have already seen, Jacob kicked his way out of the womb holding his brother's heel. Later, with the help of his mother, he stole the blessing that was intended for his older twin, Esau. It went downhill from there.

To avoid his brother's anger, Jacob fled to the land of his mother's birth. There he worked for his uncle Laban, who agreed to give him the hand of his younger daughter Rachel in exchange for seven year's labor. On the night of Jacob's wedding his uncle switched daughters. One suspects there was a lot of drinking going on! Be that as it may, when Jacob awoke in the morning he discovered that he had consummated his marriage with Leah, the elder and less beautiful daughter, not Rachel, the one he truly loved. Jacob was crafty, but Laban was craftier.

Jacob worked seven more years for the hand of Rachel. Thus Jacob was married to sisters—Leah, whom he did not love, but who was sturdy and fertile, and Rachel whom he did love, but who was fragile and barren. The dysfunction does not end here.

Leah gave birth to six sons. Rachel, who had a most difficult time getting pregnant, died giving birth to her second son. Rachel's firstborn was Joseph. When Jacob looked at Joseph, he saw Rachel, and it was obvious to all that Joseph was his father's favorite.

When he was just a lad, Jacob gave Joseph a special coat with long sleeves. One translation suggests that it was a coat of many colors. The coat made Joseph feel special and his brothers feel resentful.

In a classic case of transference, the hatred of the brothers was not directed toward the source, their father, but at their brother Joseph. They were unable to hate their father because they needed him and craved his love. They did not need Joseph. Genesis tells us, "They could not speak peaceably to him" (Genesis 37:4).

Their anger was compounded by Joseph's dreams. Initially his dreams seemed self-serving. Oblivious to his brother's feelings, he announced that he in his dream he and his brothers were all binding sheaves when his sheaf stood erect and the sheaves of the remaining eleven bowed down to his. Later Joseph shared his second dream in which the sun and the moon and eleven stars bowed down to him. At this point even his father was offended and rebuked him. "What's with all this dreaming? Am I and your mother and your brothers all supposed to bow down to you?"

One day Jacob sent Joseph to check on his older brothers who were tending sheep a far distance from their home. The brothers saw him coming from afar, the bright colors of the special coat setting him apart from the sand colored landscape. As they watched him approach, the brothers said derisively, "Here comes the dreamer!"

It is in this scene that we see the true state of the family. There is something more than a mild case of sibling rivalry going on. Nearly all parents complain that their sons are forever fighting, but this scene goes far beyond mere bickering. We learn that the brothers have been contemplating murder. Their sick reasoning goes something like this: If we get rid of the one dad loves most, he'll love us more.

Initially we have sympathy for the brothers. It is not right for a parent to treat one child better than another. We will always love our children differently, for they are different, but we can love them fairly. We can treat them fairly. The brothers lose our sympathy, however, when they plan something that is far more heinous than favoritism—murder.

Reuben, the eldest son, convinces the brothers to put Joseph in a pit rather than kill him. Later they sell him to a group of traders traveling to Egypt. The brothers kept the special coat and, after soaking it in the blood of an animal, returned it to their father. Sin has a way of escalating. What started as jealousy turned into the threat of murder, betrayal, and deceit.

When the father sees the bloody coat and assumes that Joseph is dead, however, he loves him even more. Joseph remains first in his father's heart. We learn that justice cannot be obtained by evil means. The brothers want an equal share of their father's love, but it cannot be obtained by betraying their brother. The only road to justice is the road of love.

Throughout the story of Joseph and his brothers, moral behavior is grounded in a sense of accountability to God. Joseph does the right thing because he knows that any sin is finally a sin against God. Children of God know that they answer to God. For example, Joseph refused to have sex with the wife of his master not only because it would betray his master, but because he knew that adultery is a great sin and evil against God.

A father decided to "take" some two-by-fours from a construction site near his home. He had his young daughter stand at the road and act as a lookout. As the father began to load the lumber into his truck, the little girl called out, "Daddy, someone's looking." The father nervously glanced around, saw no one, and continued to lift two-by-fours into the truck. The daughter gave the same warning a second and then a third time before the father finally said, "I don't see anyone. Who is looking?" The girl answered, "God is looking, daddy."

Christians assume that God is looking. We are accountable. How can we sin and do evil in the sight of God? God has given us life and love and forgiveness. Honesty and integrity are ways of saying thanks for all we have received.

Bible stories are never just about human beings. They are always about God and how God works in and through our lives. What can't be seen at first in Joseph's story is that the source of Joseph's dreams is God. What can't be seen at first is the hidden way in which God works through the lives of people, even dysfunctional people. What can't be seen is that God, the giver of dreams, never gives a dream to benefit just one person. Rather, God's dreams are for the family, for the community, and for the nation. It is a dream that will provide *shalom*, the word we so inadequately translate as peace.

*Shalom* is how Jewish people greet each other upon meeting and parting. The best translation for *shalom* is total well-being. *Shalom* is a state of wholeness, fullness of health, joy, and prosperity, as well as peace. It is never seen merely in individualistic terms. It is a gift offered through one person to the community. The gift God gave Joseph was the gift God used to bless all the families of the earth.

God chose Joseph not to honor him, but to love and save Israel through him. God chose him in order that he could be a blessing. God chose Joseph to be his instrument of *shalom*. God chose the younger to save the older. This is but one of a series of surprises. God frequently uses the weak to instruct the strong, the foolish to reveal truth to the wise, the disabled to bring health to the able-bodied, and the aged to bring gifts to us all. A true test of our ability to be in touch with God is our care for the fragile and weak in this world. Bible stories tell us never to ignore anyone, particularly strangers, because God comes incognito, with many aliases.

Joseph was able to identify and listen to God. He lived with a deep sense of the presence of God. Joseph listened to his dreams, which he knew to be the voice of God. His deep God-consciousness led him to believe with Paul, who lived fourteen hundred years later, that "all things work together for good for those who love God, who are called according to his purpose" (Romans 8:28).

# { beautiful on the inside }

*And David said, "Blessed be GOD, the God of Israel. He sent you to meet me! And blessed be your good sense! Bless you for keeping me from murder and taking charge of looking out for me. A close call!"*
—*1 Samuel 25:32-33*, The Message

It has been said that beauty is only skin deep. With respect to physical beauty, that is obviously true, but inner beauty runs deep, all the way to the heart, all the way to the spirit. Physical beauty in a man or a woman is a wonderful gift, but inner beauty is a gift of the spirit. It is a grace.

The story of David and Abigail is a story about inner strength, inner courage, and inner beauty. It is a story that tells us how such humble gifts can change individuals and transform societies.

For a period of David's life, when he was trying to avoid the death threats of King Saul, he lived with a band of men in a kind of Robin Hood-like existence. The group lived off the land and provided security for villages from marauding bands of outlaws in exchange for food and a modest amount of money. David and his men did this quietly because they had to avoid the armies of Saul that were searching for them.

One of the men whom David protected was Nabal, a wealthy landowner, who had trouble with bands of outlaws stealing his sheep and kidnapping his worker's wives. Nabal, which means "fool," had the reputation for being surly and mean. David and his men provided security for him at a reasonable price. People said the service was honest, which meant David's men did not steal anything while they were providing protection. David was so effective that the problems ceased, and Nabal's wealth grew.

One day David heard that Nabal was throwing a feast for his people celebrating the end of the sheep shearing. David sent some of his men to Nabal and asked politely if he and his men might share in the festivities. Nabal turned on David's men and sneered, "Who is this David? Who is this son of Jesse? The country is full of runaway servants these days. Do you think I'm going to take good bread and wine . . . and give it to men I've never laid eyes on?" (1 Samuel 25:10-11, *The Message)*. It was quite an insult.

When David's men returned and repeated Nabal's words, David was furious. "Okay, men," he shouted, "strap on your swords." David, whose band of men numbered four hundred, had decided to pay Nabal a visit.

Meanwhile, one of Nabal's servants who had overheard the conversation ran to tell Nabal's wife, the beautiful Abigail:

> David sent messengers from the backcountry to salute our master, but he tore into them with insults. Yet these men treated us very well. They took nothing from us and didn't take advantage of us all the time we were in the fields. They formed a wall around us, protecting us day and night all the time we were out tending the sheep. Do something quickly because big trouble is ahead for our master and all of us. Nobody can talk to him. He's impossible—a real brute!
> —1 Samuel 25:14-17, *The Message*

It didn't take long for Abigail to act. She gathered together as much food as she could lay hands on in a few short minutes, including bread, wine, meat, bushels of roasted grain, raisins, and figs. She loaded them on pack animals and, with a few servants, rode off into the backcountry to find David.

As David rode, his anger increased. He had been ridiculed and now planned to wreak his own vengeance. "God strike me dead," he shouted, "if I don't kill every last one of those men before morning."

On his way to bloody revenge, however, David met courage and inner beauty in the person of Abigail. When Abigail found David she quickly dismounted, threw herself to the ground and appealed to David's highest nature. She begged forgiveness for her foolish husband, who unfortunately had lived up to his name. She reminded David gently that he was a believer, and that faith in God has wonderful and terrifying consequences, among which is that we refrain from playing God. Vengeance belongs to God. Abigail knew that David could wipe out all of Nabal's village and still go up in the popularity polls. Society would understand, but not God. She reminded David that when you deal with God you are dealing with a higher set of rules.

She said, "It is the Lord who has kept you from taking revenge and killing your enemies." Perhaps, but God was speaking through Abigail. David had forgotten God, just as we often forget God when we decide to right wrongs on our own. How difficult it is to not try to get even. How difficult it is to let God take care of the balance sheet. "Vengeance is mine, I will repay, says the Lord" (Romans 12:19). It is difficult to remember that.

Abigail put her own life on the line to prevent violence. Many a woman has stood between the anger of a man and, say, a child, and has been seriously injured. Many a woman has stood up for someone and has been battered. Abigail the beautiful was also Abigail the courageous. Abigail, like all peace warriors, took a risk, but the risk was smaller because she had accurately read the heart of David. She knew that he was a man of deep faith. It is not that people of faith never get angry or seek revenge, it's just that when you appeal to their faith commitments your chances of a positive response are better. Abigail appealed to David's faith in God, and did so in humility. In the words of Eugene Peterson, "Abigail on her knees put David on his knees."

Like all great leaders, David was susceptible to arrogance. At this moment, David was so full of himself that he was willing to kill over a snub. He ignored his faith in God and was about to take matters into his own hands. Abigail reminded him who he was and what he stood for. To David's credit, when right was laid before him, he recognized it and acted on it. He expressed his appreciation to Abigail, "Bless you for keeping me from murder and taking charge of looking out for me. A close call! As GOD lives, the God of Israel who kept me from hurting you, if you had not come as quickly as you did, stopping me in my tracks, by morning there would have been nothing left of Nabal . . ." (1 Samuel 25:33-34, *The Message).*

All of us need an Abigail in our lives. We need someone to remind us of the consequences of our faith and of the convictions we hold. That happens most frequently when we are in a relationship where we give permission to someone to love us and challenge us—which is often the same thing. To be accountable to God, it helps to be accountable to someone in our lives—a friend, a pastor, Bible study partners, a loved one. They can save us from disastrous actions.

People in high places often get into difficulty when they isolate themselves. People with power rarely give others permission to challenge them. They no longer have anyone who feels as if they can act like Abigail.

Parents are to be an Abigail to their children. When I was about to take the car for the first time for an out-of-town date, my mother said, "Remember who you are." I thought, "Mom, you don't have to say that." But she did. It is what all parents are to do. At some point the roles are reversed, and children remind their parents who they are. As adults, however, if we have no one to challenge us it is usually because we have given no one permission to challenge and love us. We all need an Abigail, someone to speak the word of God to us and remind us who we are.

Nabal, like many fools, died young. Abigail had asked David to remember her. He not only remembered her, he found her after her husband's death and married her.

Abigail can be a great model for us, but our greatest model is Christ, who is patient and kind, not jealous or boastful, not arrogant or rude. People who imitate Christ end up with a beauty that does not remain skin deep but goes straight to the soul.

# { a clean heart }

*But GOD was not at all pleased with what David had done, and sent Nathan to David.*
    —*2 Samuel 12:1,* The Message

The name David means beloved. In the early chapters of 1 Samuel, David lived up to his name. He was brave, faithful, and charming. The people both loved and adored him. In their eyes he could do no wrong. Under his leadership the country grew, the arts flourished, and pride returned to an embattled people.

Part of David's charm was that he was a man of deep faith. He was a favorite of the priests and formed a guild of poets who wrote religious songs for all occasions. Those songs have been collected and preserved in the book we now call "Psalms."

Many rulers face new difficulties when they remain in power for an extended period of time. Some of their problems take place because the longer they rule, the more isolated they become. The longer they breathe the rarified air of the head of state, the greater the temptation to live without accountability. The longer David ruled, the more he distanced himself from the people and even his own army.

Our story begins with these ominous words: "In the spring of the year, the time when kings go out to battle, David sent Joab [his general] with his officers and all Israel with him; they ravaged the Ammonites, and besieged Rabbah. But David remained at Jerusalem" (2 Samuel 11:1).

In the early days when he was a new king, David fought *with* his soldiers; now they fought for him while he remained at home. While his men were in battle, David strolled on his balcony where, on an adjoining roof, he saw a beautiful woman bathing. David immediately enquired about the woman and was told that she was Bathsheba, daughter of Eliam, the wife of Uriah the Hittite. That ought to have been enough information to keep David away, but it was not. Even though she was the wife of a soldier under his command, David invited her to the palace, and lay with her. The account of this union is rather crass. There is no hint of love or affection. There is not even a record of conversation. It was pure lust, and lust often comes with a price.

David was soon to get the bill, for Bathsheba sent a message with three little words. They were not those wonderful words, *I love you*, but the words, *I am pregnant*.

Terror gripped the heart of David. Adultery was a serious enough crime but David magnified the crime with a cover-up. In an attempt to make it appear that Bathsheba was impregnated by her husband, Uriah, David brought him back from the front. It was a crass and disgusting move. It could only work, however, if Uriah slept with his wife.

Unfortunately for David, Uriah refused. A convert to the Jewish faith, Uriah was too disciplined to sleep in the luxury of his own bed when his fellow soldiers were in the midst of a battle. Uriah the convert, not David the king, was the principled man. After two failed attempts to get Uriah to go home, David took him out drinking, and then sent him back into battle the next day with a message for the general. He ordered Joab, the field general, to put Uriah where the fighting was the most fierce. It was not long before the enemy took care of David's problem. Uriah was killed. David had now broken three commandments. He coveted another's wife, he committed adultery, and he had a man murdered.

When Uriah died, Bathsheba mourned for her dead husband. When the mourning period was over, David sent for her and married her. She gave birth to a son.

Years ago a married man told me how he had been involved with several different women. I knew him as a good man from a good background. I asked him, "How did you live with the guilt?"

He told me that he had felt no guilt. "I was totally blind to what I was doing. Now I see it. Then I didn't."

How do decent people get involved in indecent behavior? One of the answers to this complicated question is, "They just don't see it." David didn't. It took a visit from a prophet, a spiritual ophthalmologist, to correct his failing eyesight. The prophet, Nathan, removed the cataracts from David's moral eyes with a story that proved to be far more powerful than a laser. It is in 2 Samuel 12:2-4 *(The Message,* paraphrased):

"There was a rich man who had many flocks and herds and a poor man who had a single lamb who grew up as a household pet," Nathan began. "When company came to the rich man's house, he didn't take a lamb from his flock, rather he took the pet from the poor man and served it for lunch."

Righteous anger arose in David, and he issued the death sentence, "As the Lord lives the man who has done this should die."

Nathan retorted, "You are the man. You have committed adultery and you have killed Uriah the Hittite with the sword, taking his wife to be your wife. Why have you despised the word of the Lord?"

That is the issue, isn't it? David despised the word, the command of God. As sure as he sinned against Uriah, David sinned against God, the God who had blessed him, who had given him everything, and was willing to give more.

Nathan knew that such behavior brings on trouble. It is not that God had to send trouble to the house of David. David's actions had sowed the seeds of dissension, ill will, envy . . . the list goes on. David did not harvest the active justice of God; he had, by his own choices, well prepared the soil for the passive justice of God. David's haughty, arrogant behavior produced a harvest of trouble, pain, and suffering for many.

Nathan words were true. A film of David's sons and daughters, children born to different wives, would be R-rated. A son by one wife raped a daughter by another. The girl's full brother avenged his sister's rape by killing the half-brother. That same son overthrew his father, sending David fleeing to the wilderness. The golden age had turned into "The Young and the Restless."

At the end of the section on the Ten Commandments in Luther's *Small Catechism* we are asked, "What does God say of all these commandments?" Luther answers from scripture:

> I the LORD your God am a jealous God, punishing children for the iniquity of parents, to the third and fourth generation of those who reject me, but showing steadfast love to the thousandth generation of those who love me and keep my commandments.
> —Deuteronomy 5:9-10

For a long time I wondered why God would punish me for what my father did. Later, I realized that this is simply a description of the way things are. What parents do or don't do has consequences not only for themselves, but for their children and perhaps even their children's children. One young boy recently told a counselor that he didn't know any male adults in his family who didn't abuse women. Abusive behavior, addictive behavior, and philandering reach far beyond the current moment. They can even touch the lives of our children and grandchildren. We know this. Our moral commitments, or lack of moral commitments, affect those who follow after us.

David heard Nathan. Scales fell from the eyes of the king, and for the first time he saw. He bowed his head and confessed, "I have sinned." He did not equivocate. He did not stonewall. He did not evade. Though it was a bit late, he confessed.

David's life had started out so positively. He was faithful, gracious and kind. Then he took his eyes off the goal, and no longer acted like a servant of God. He began to believe that he was bigger than life itself. He no longer felt accountable to his family, his country, or his Lord.

Though there is very little good news in this story, a thread of hope remains. David did not have to accept Nathan's pronouncement. As king he could have ridiculed the prophet or he could have done what Herod did when John the Baptist challenged him—jailed him and had him killed. He did not. He honored and heeded the word that came from God through Nathan. Even a tardy act of repentance is better than no repentance at all—it opens the door to forgiveness and second chances.

Here is where we see the power of the gospel. David asked for God's mercy and received it. It is never too late to seek forgiveness. The Ash Wednesday liturgy boldly declares that, "God does not desire the death of sinners, but rather that they may turn from their wickedness and live." David no longer claimed moral autonomy. He bent his will to the rule of God.

Tradition tells us that as an act of penance David wrote Psalm 51:

> Create in me a clean heart O God,
>     and put a new and right spirit within me.
> Do not cast me away from your presence,
>     and do not take your holy spirit from me.
> Restore to me the joy of your salvation,
>     and sustain in me a willing spirit.
>     —Psalm 51:10-12

A number of people have compared this story to former President Clinton's encounter with Monica Lewinsky. I think that is a stretch. David's situation is far more serious. More important, however, if we immediately link the ex-President, or anyone else to this story, we have failed to understand the real point—which is to find ourselves. These stories have not been given so that we can point at others. They are gifts to us to help open *our* eyes so *we* can see. They are reminders not of the consequences of someone else's sin, but of our own.

Though our sins may not be as dramatic as David's, they can become just as serious if we stubbornly fail to confess them and seek forgiveness. In today's world, we even resist the word sin itself. We fail to call sin what it is, a black spot on our lives that separates us from our neighbors and from God. What is so sad is that our failure to confess and repent means we deny ourselves the gift of God's love and mercy. Remember: "If we confess our sins, [God] who is faithful and just will forgive us our sins and cleanse us from all unrighteousness" (1 John 1:9).

# { a dip in the creek }

*[Naaman's] servants caught up with him and said, "Father, if the*
*prophet had asked you to do something hard and heroic, wouldn't*
*you have done it? So why not this simple 'wash and be clean'?"*
—2 Kings 5:13, The Message

Naaman, commander of the armies of Syria, was the Colin Powell of his day. He was a brave warrior and a successful general. Unfortunately, he had leprosy, a terrible skin disease. Naaman's wife had a Jewish servant girl who told her that there was a prophet in Israel who could cure her husband of his disease.

Desperate to be healed, Naaman immediately approached his king, and told him what the servant had said. The king told him to go to Israel, and he wrote a letter to the king of Israel asking him to see to Naaman's cure. Did the king of Syria write his letter to allow his commander to travel Jewish roads without it being seen as an act of war? Or did he write the letter because he believed the world works from the top down? I think it is the latter, and it runs against the theme of this story, which is that that God's world works in the opposite direction, from the bottom up.

If you go the Mayo Clinic in Rochester, Minnesota, to see a specialist, you don't have to pave the way by talking to your good friend the governor of Minnesota, or the mayor the city. In order to see the prophet you talk to God, not the king.

Give Naaman credit for this: At the advice of his wife's servant, he went to Israel. When he arrived at the palace, the king panicked. He thought the letter from the king of Syria was an ultimatum: Heal the general or you'll face war with Syria.

Fortunately for the king, the prophet Elisha took him off the hook. When he heard of Naaman's arrival he sent a note to the king saying, "Send him to me. I'll take care of it."

Here is where the story gets interesting. Naaman arrived at the home of Elisha with a huge caravan of people and gifts. Like many if not most important people, the commander expected the prophet to rush out and greet him like, well, an important person. Elisha, however, stayed in his little house and sent a servant with these instructions, "Go, wash in the Jordan seven times, and your flesh shall be restored and you shall be clean" (2 Kings 5:10). Naaman was furious.

When I was at the Mayo Clinic in Rochester, Minnesota, I was told that a sultan from the Middle East had arrived that morning to be treated. Imagine if instead of a world famous specialist an intern greeted him and said, "Take two aspirin, and a forty minute swim in the Mississippi. Have a nice day!"

Naaman expected two things: personal attention, and a fancy healing service. He got neither. "I thought that for me he would surely come out," complained Naaman. I thought he would "stand and call on the name of the LORD his God, and would wave his hand over the spot, and cure the leprosy" (2 Kings 5:11).

Instead, Naaman received instructions to dip seven times in a creek, the tiny Jordan River. This command pushed him over the edge. To paraphrase him, Naaman shouted, "We've got better rivers back home. If I bathed in one of our rivers at least I'd get clean. I'm not about to go dipping in that mud hole they call the Jordan."

In the eyes of the rich and famous, Biblical religion has never measured up. It has always been a bit low brow. Old Testament prophets were rough and crude. Jesus was born of an unwed teenage mother. His disciples were unschooled fishermen and tax collectors.

In the Bible it is the little people, the servants, who most frequently get the point. Naaman's servant approached his master and said, "Father, if the prophet had commanded you to do something difficult, would you not have done it? How much more, when all he said to you was, 'Wash, and be clean'?" (2 Kings 5:13).

The servant was right, of course. If Elisha had put the commander on a rigorous six-month exercise program, changed his diet, and commanded him to pray an hour each day, he probably would have done it without blinking. Instead, he told him to do something simple and he was offended.

Reluctantly, Naaman did what Elisha and his servant told him to do. He washed seven times in the muddy Jordan, and he was healed. Could we say that Naaman humbled himself and so opened himself to the gifts of God?

If you sought help in saving or strengthening your marriage, a counselor could teach you elaborate skills in personal communication and invite you back for seven more sessions. You'd probably do it. Or she could say to you, "Spend four minutes a day with your spouse praying out loud for each other." In many cases it could have the same effect. Would you prefer the difficult or the simple exercise? A few minutes of prayer each day works wonders in marriage, and yet people don't do it.

Do you want to make a difference in a person's life? Send them a hand-written note of five sentences to tell them how much you care. If this sounds sappy it is because you haven't sent one or received one lately.

When Naaman was healed, he offered a number of expensive gifts to the prophet. Again, it is interesting to speculate about motives. Did he make the offer out of gratitude, or to pay for his healing? Whatever his reason, Elijah would have none of it. He turned the gifts down cold. He was announcing that his kind of healing is sheer grace. It was offered with no strings attached. There is no repaying God. There is only thanking God. Thanking is primarily what worship is all about. After we hear those great words, "I declare to you the entire forgiveness of all your sins," we respond with songs of praise and gratitude.

At this point of the story, Naaman starts to get it. When Elisha turned down his gift, Naaman didn't protest. He was beginning to see that it was indeed all about grace. He knew that he would still have to serve his king, a man who worshiped a false god, but he also knew that from that day forward he could only pray to Yahweh.

There is one more set of lessons for Naaman and the rest of us to learn. These lessons aren't found in the story. In this story, it was important for Naaman to learn that God can and does answer prayer. The next lesson is to learn that God frequently answers in a way different from the one we wanted and hoped for. This is when we learn that God is not our errand boy, nor a genii who can be manipulated into granting wishes contrary to his will. Ours is a God we can trust to answer our prayers in the best possible way, even if the answer is no. God always has the big picture in mind. We seldom do.

A few years ago Chicago's Cardinal Bernadin announced that he had cancer and it was terminal. He had been praying for healing and he was working for healing. He was following his doctor's orders exactly, and unexpectedly, in mid-August he was given a clean bill of health. By early September, however, it all turned around; the doctors had bad news. The cardinal had less than a year to live.

The media—who had earlier put the accusations of a young man who said the cardinal had sexually abused him on page one, and then buried the retraction deep in the paper when the accusations proved to be false—had a feeding frenzy. One columnist asked him, "Does this mean God isn't answering your prayer?"

The cardinal said that God had answered the prayer, just not as he had hoped. For the next year, he wrote and taught, and his impact was tremendous. The cardinal called his cancer a "special gift" from God, which is to say that he saw his cancer as a part of God's grace. Grace not only gives us sight when we are blind and helps us find the way when we are lost, but grace makes it possible to face our last days in peace and joy. The cardinal believed that his cancer gave him an opportunity to reach people he had never reached before. In the end he believed that the answer he received was better than the answer he sought. When God is involved it always is.

# questions for further reflection on telling the story

1. Abraham was not called to talk about God, to convert people, or to build temples, but he was called to live in the blessing of God, to practice his faith, and to allow the kingdom of God to work through him. What does it mean to live in the blessing of God? How does someone practice the faith? How do we allow the kingdom of God to work through us?

2. What shape has the blessing of God taken in your life? How often are you aware of your blessing?

3. To whom have you given permission to love and challenge you? How did you give that person permission?

4. Initially, what was it that prevented Naaman from being healed? What are other things that stand in the way of people being healed?

# { notes }

1. I have gained a great deal from Robert Enright's book *Forgiveness Is a Choice* (Washington, D.C.: American Psychological Association, 2001).
2. Siegel, Bernie S., M.D., *Love, Medicine and Miracles: Lessons Learned about Self-Healing from a Surgeon's Experience with Exceptional Patients* (New York: Harper and Row, 1995), 180.
3. Kozol, Jonathan, *Amazing Grace: The Lives of Children and the Conscience of a Nation* (New York: HarperCollins, 1986), 78.
4. Hunter, James Davison, "God's Long Range Plan," *The Death of Character* (New York: Basic Books, 2000), xv.
5. Hillerman, Tony, *Sacred Clowns* (New York: HarperTorch, 1993), 16.
6. Fryer, Kelly A., *Reclaiming the "L" Word: Renewing the Church from Its Lutheran Core* (Minneapolis: Augsburg Fortress, 2003). A few years ago our congregation chose this text as our fall study book. Those who have read her fine book will recognize my debt to her for several of the ideas found here.
7. Bonhoeffer, Dietrich, *Letters and Papers from Prison,* New greatly enlarged edition (London: S.C.M. Press, Ltd., 1953, 1967, 1971), 347–48.